THE GIANT BOOK OF CLASSICAL MUSIC

68 of the World's Most Beloved Masterpieces in Their Original Form

Selected and Edited by E. L. LANCASTER and KENON D. RENFROW

Alfred Music
P.O. Box 10003
Van Nuys, CA 91410-0003
alfred.com

ISBN-10: 0-7390-7346-X
ISBN-13: 978-0-7390-7346-9

Piano keys: © Shutterstock.com / Ensuper • Brush stroke: © Shutterstock.com / foxie • Beethoven (plaster bust): © Shutterstock.com / Brendan Howard

Contents by Composer

Contents by Title

Tango in D Major

(España)

Isaac Albéniz (1860–1909)
Op. 165, No. 2

Solfeggio in C Minor

Carl Philipp Emanuel Bach
(1714–1788)

Invention No. 8 in F Major

Johann Sebastian Bach (1685–1750)
BWV 779

Invention No. 13 in A Minor

Johann Sebastian Bach (1685–1750)

BWV 714

Invention No. 14 in B-flat Major

Johann Sebastian Bach (1685–1750)
BWV 785

Prelude in C Major

(The Well-Tempered Clavier, Book 1)

Johann Sebastian Bach (1685–1750)

BWV 846

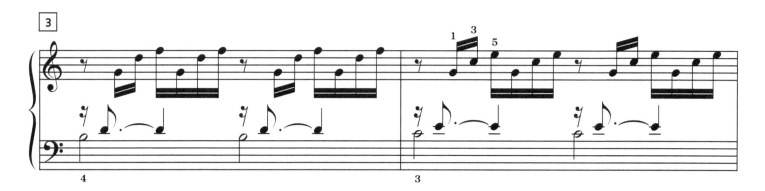

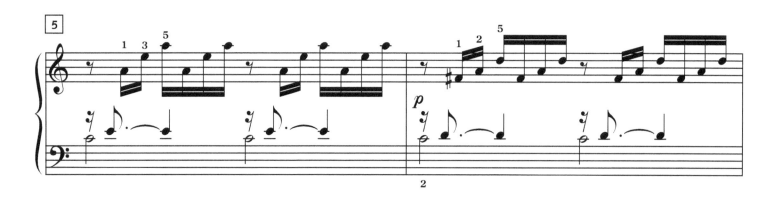

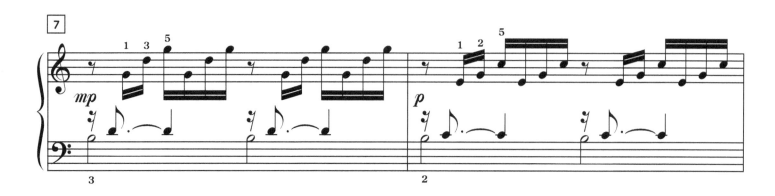

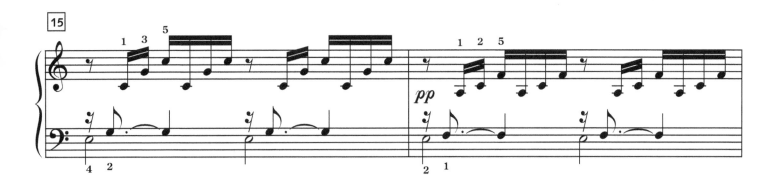

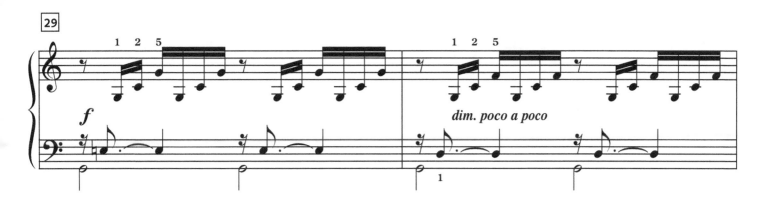

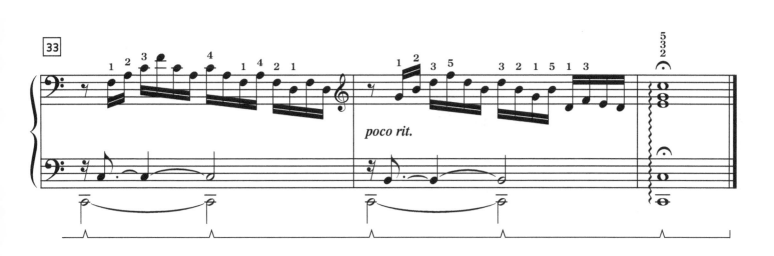

Bear Dance

Béla Bartók
(1881-1945)

Für Elise

Ludwig van Beethoven (1770-1827)
WoO 59

Sonata No. 8 in C Minor

(Pathétique)

(Movement II)

Ludwig van Beethoven (1770-1827)

Op. 13

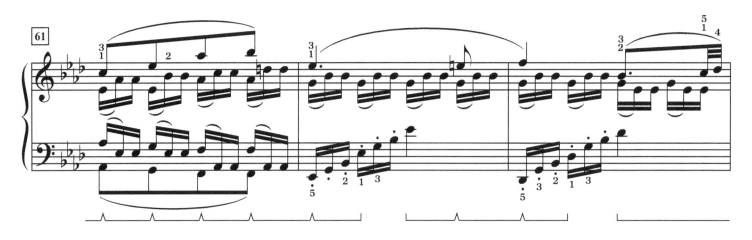

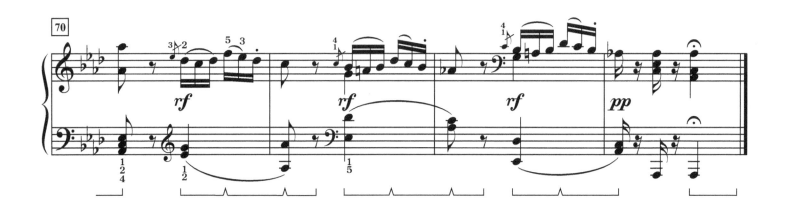

Sonata No. 14 in C-sharp Minor

(Moonlight)

(Movement I)

Ludwig van Beethoven (1770-1827)
Op. 27, No. 2

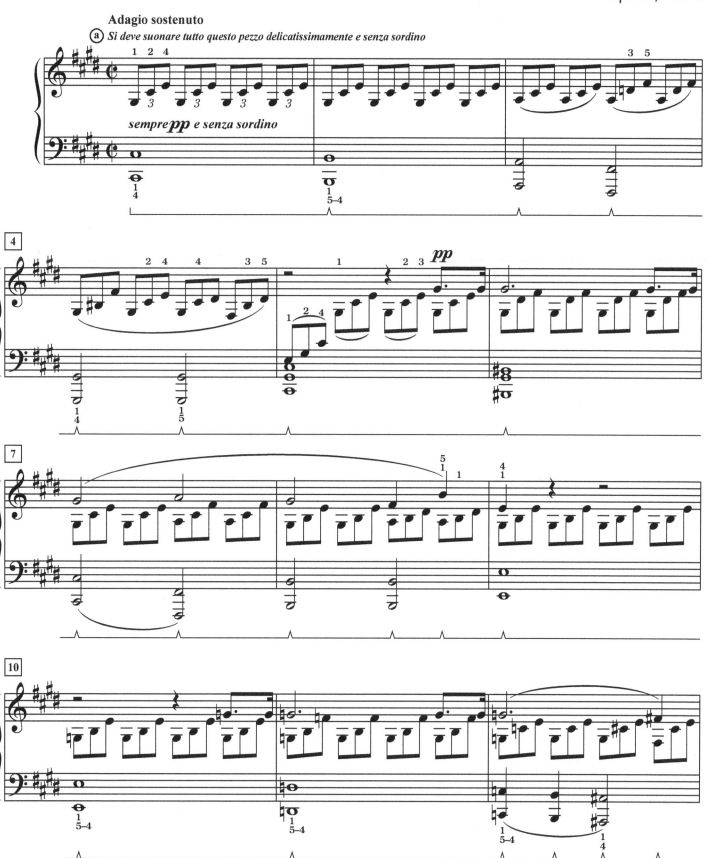

a This whole piece must be played with the greatest delicacy and with pedal.

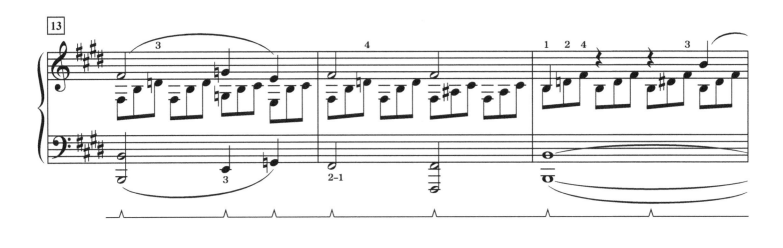

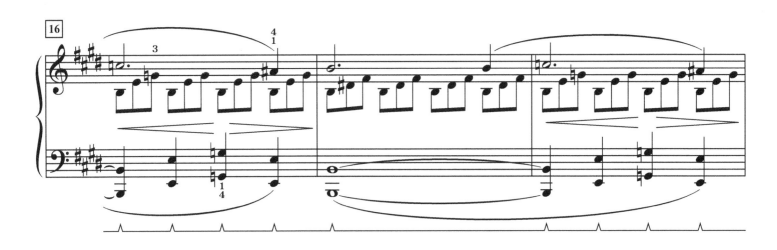

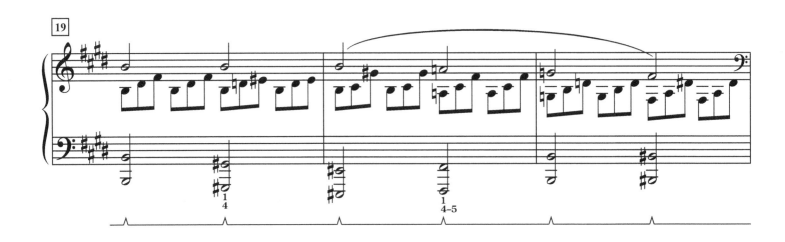

Menuet in G Major

Ludwig van Beethoven (1770-1827)
WoO 10, No. 2

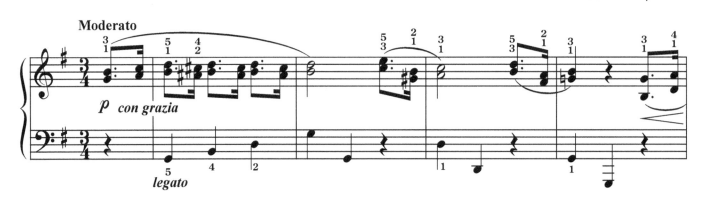

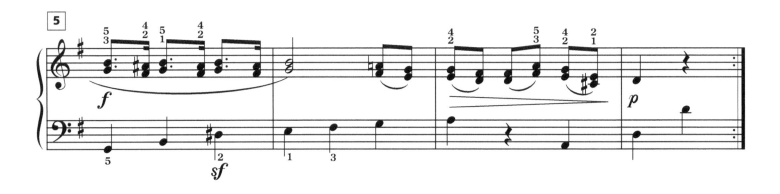

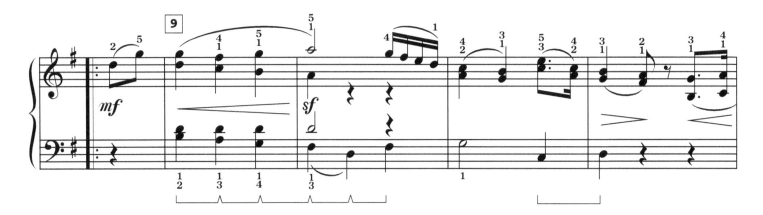

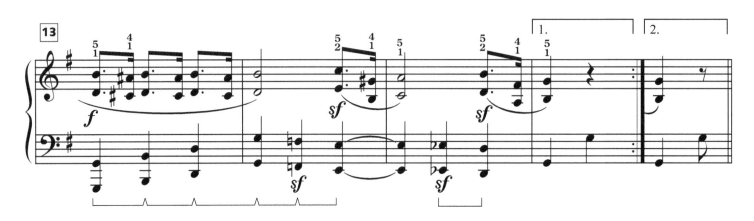

Trio

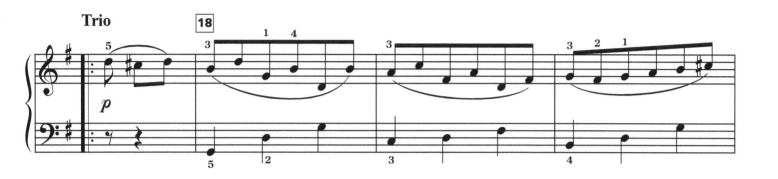

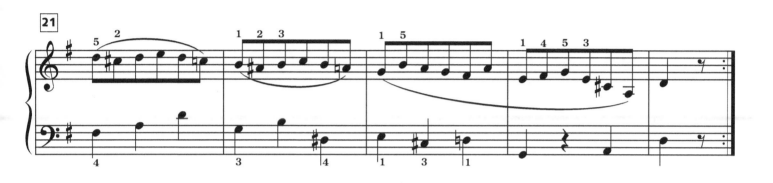

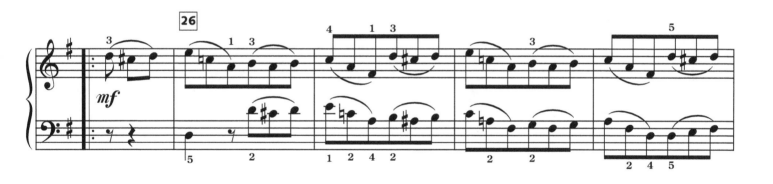

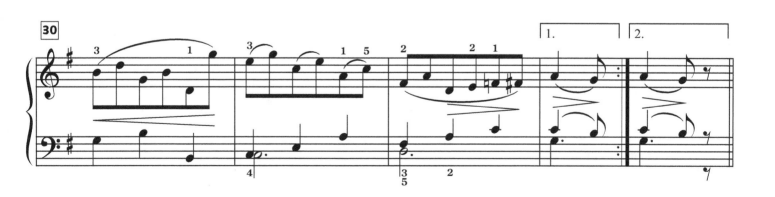

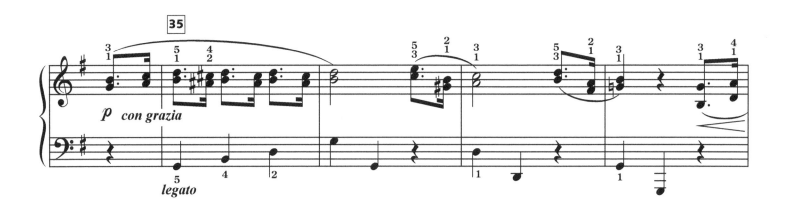

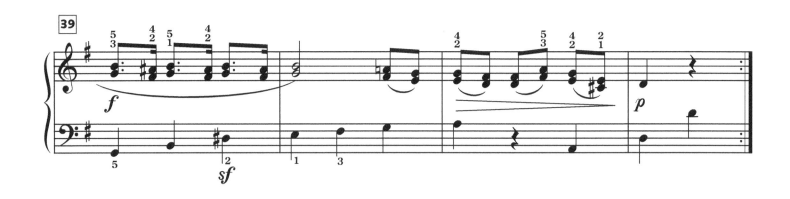

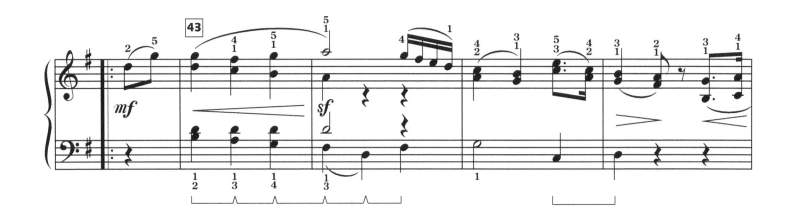

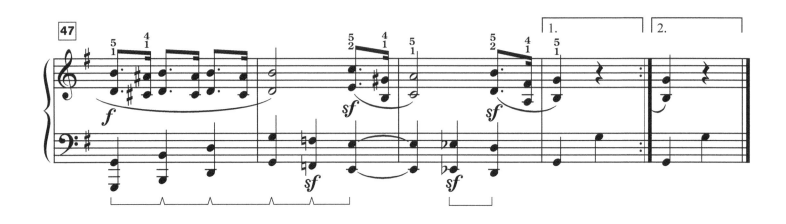

Twelfth Street Rag

Euday Louis Bowman
(1887-1949)

Ballade

Johann Burgmüller (1806-1874)
Op. 100, No. 15

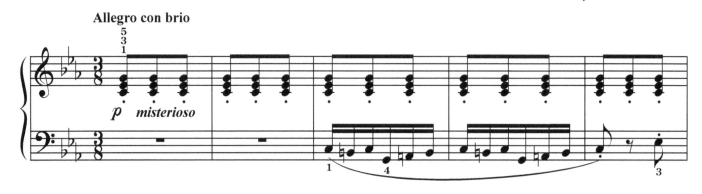

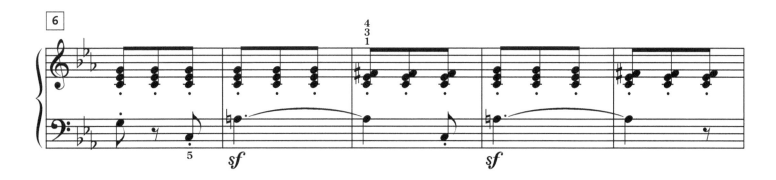

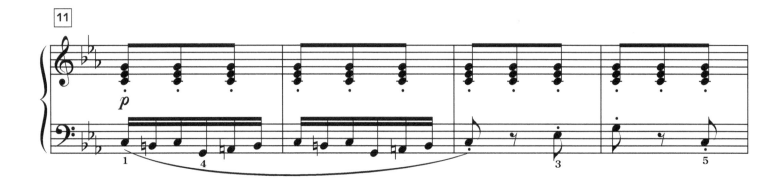

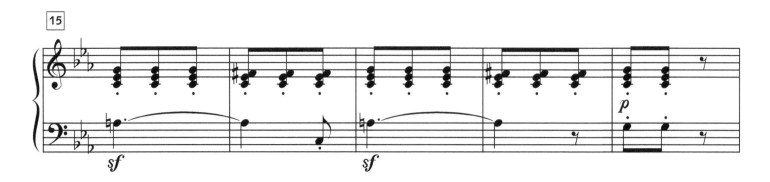

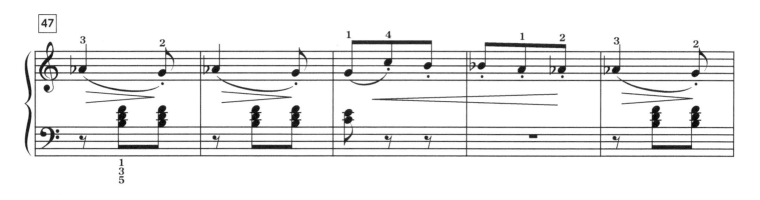

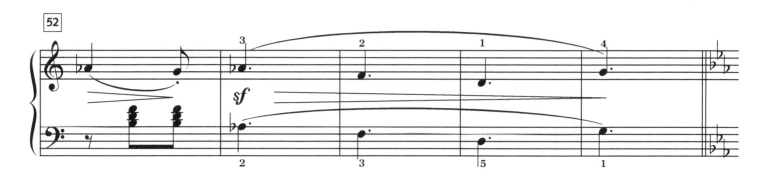

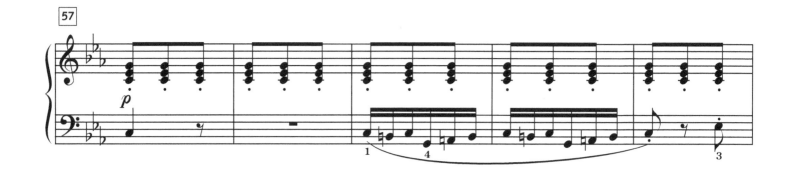

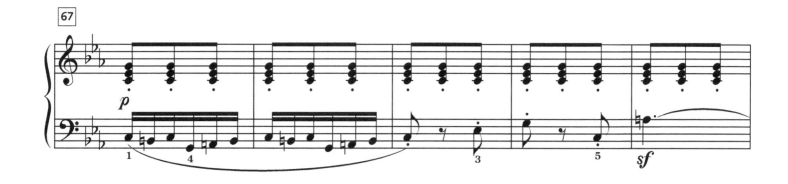

Waltz in A-flat Major

Johannes Brahms (1833-1897)
Op. 39, No. 15

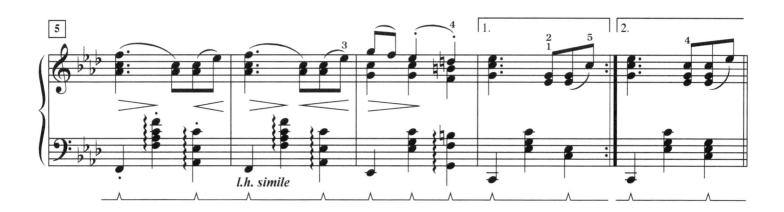

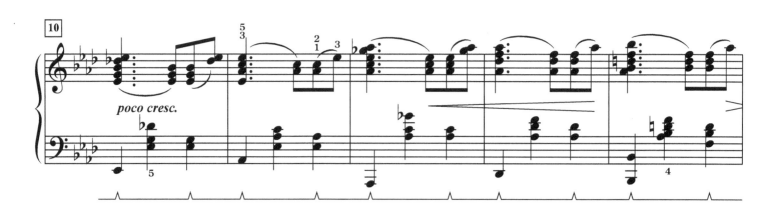

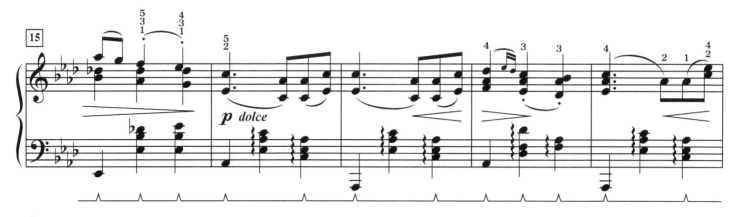

ⓐ Tempo marking is editorial. Brahms gave no tempo indication.

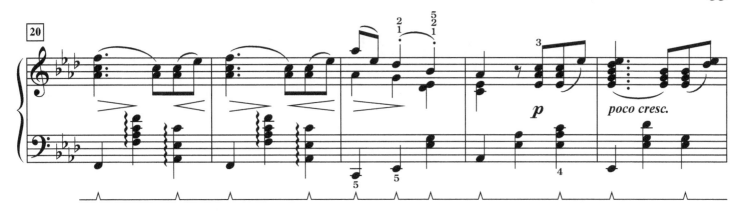

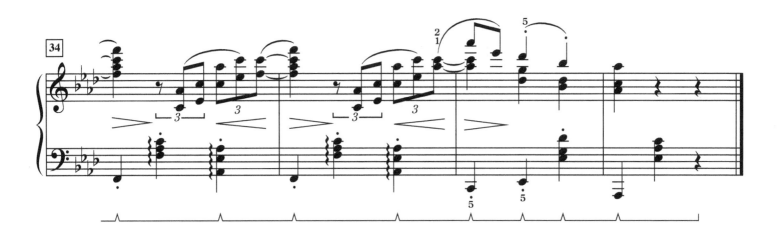

Waltz in E Major

Johannes Brahms (1833-1897)
Op. 39, No. 2

ⓐ Tempo marking is editorial. Brahms gave no tempo indication.

Nocturne in E Minor

Frédéric Chopin (1810-1849)
Op. 72, No. 1

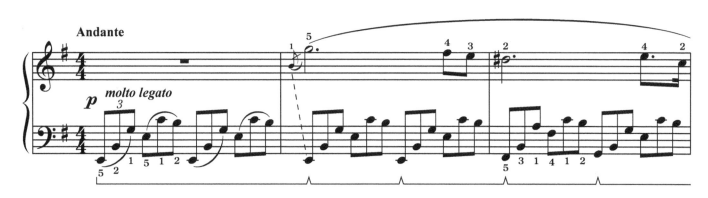

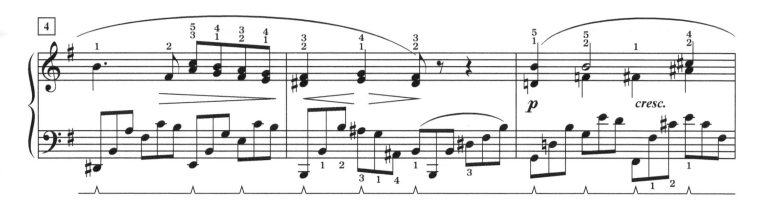

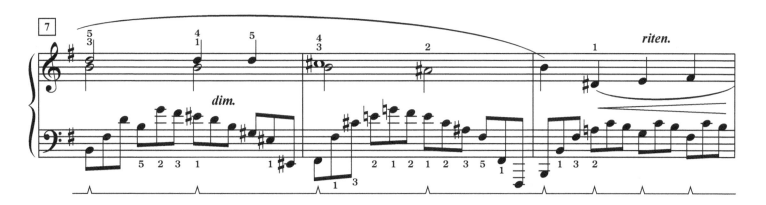

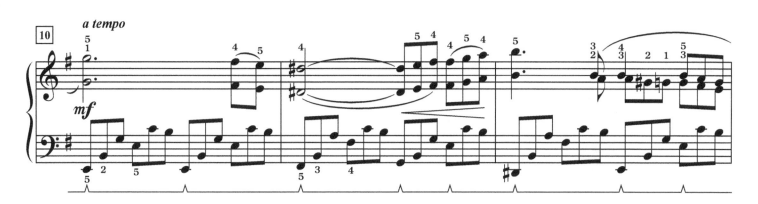

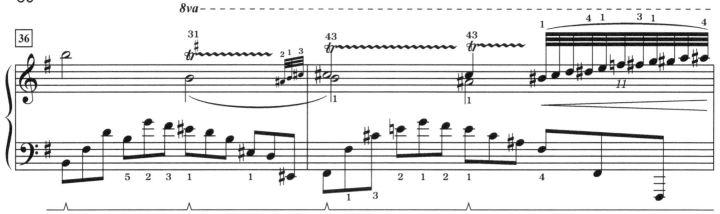

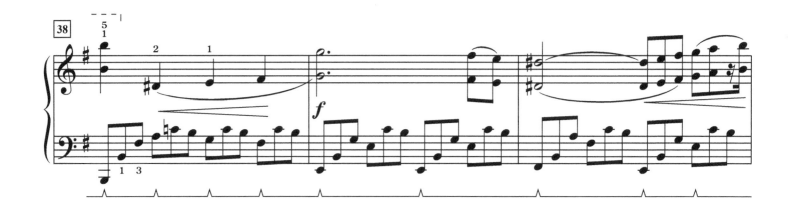

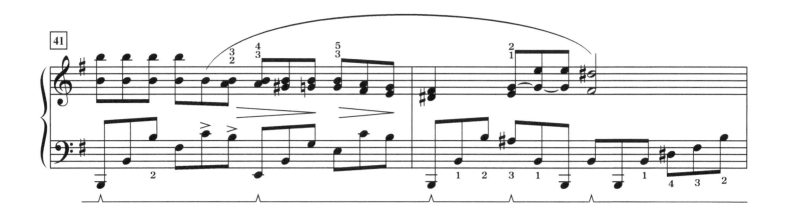

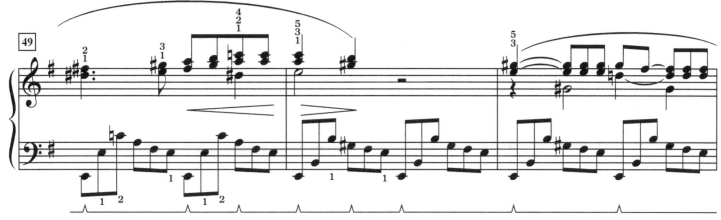

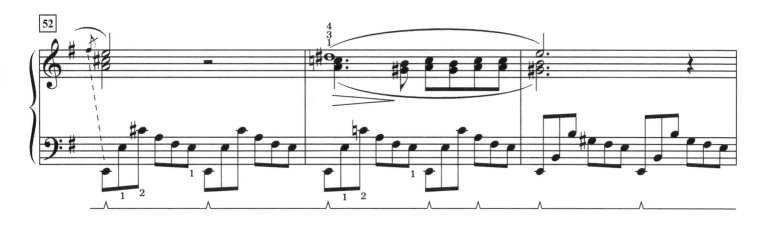

Nocturne in E-flat Major

Frédéric Chopin (1810-1849)
Op. 9, No. 2

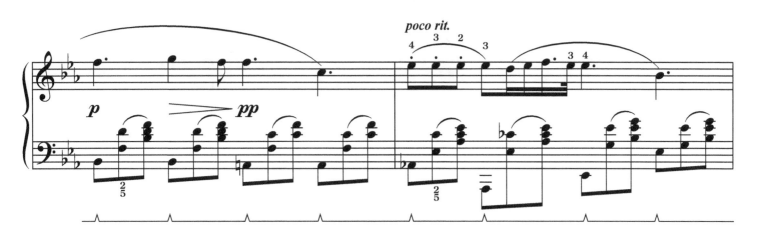

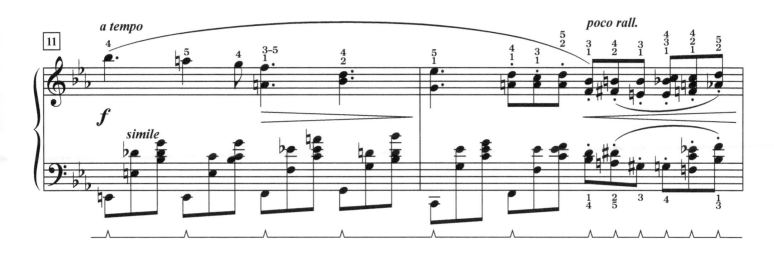

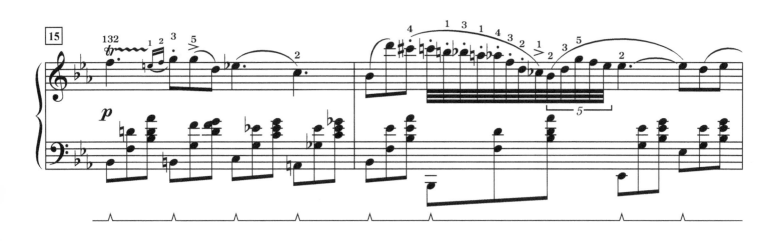

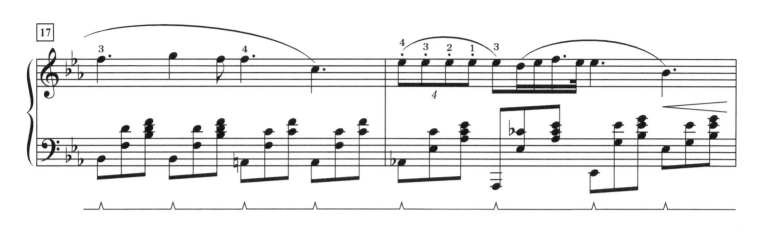

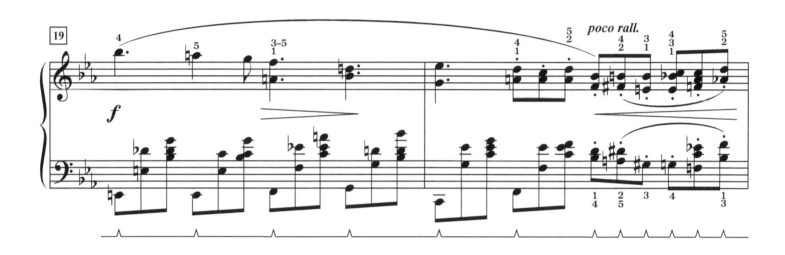

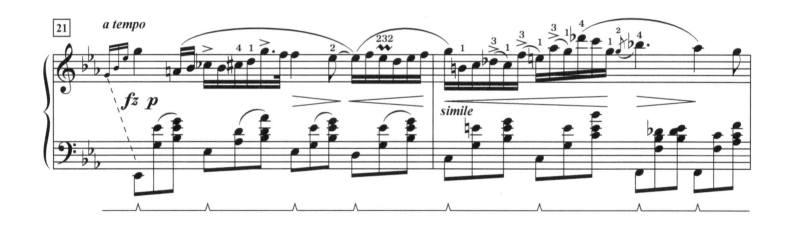

Prelude in E Minor

Frédéric Chopin (1810-1849)
Op. 28, No. 4

Prelude in A Major

Frédéric Chopin (1810-1849)
Op. 28, No. 7

Prelude in C Minor

Frédéric Chopin (1810-1849)
Op. 28, No. 20

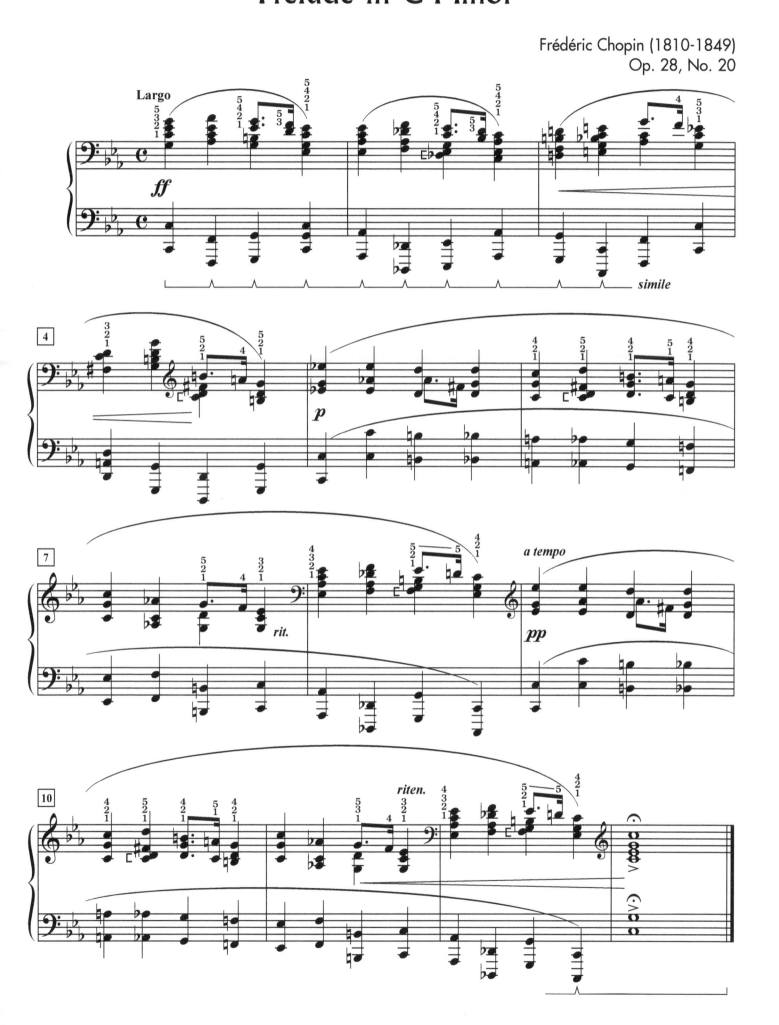

Waltz in D-flat Major
(Minute)

Frédéric Chopin (1810-1849)
Op. 64, No. 1

Sonatina in C Major

(Movements I, II & III)

Muzio Clementi (1753-1832)
Op. 36, No. 1

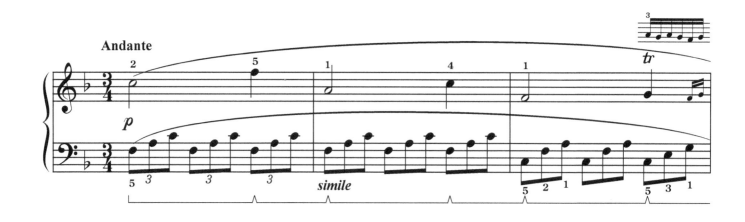

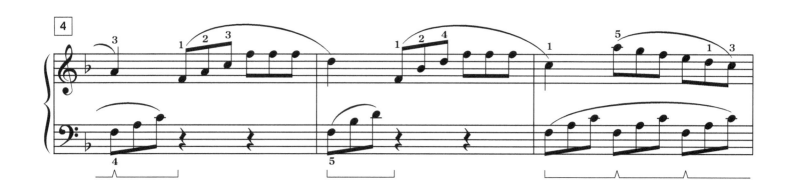

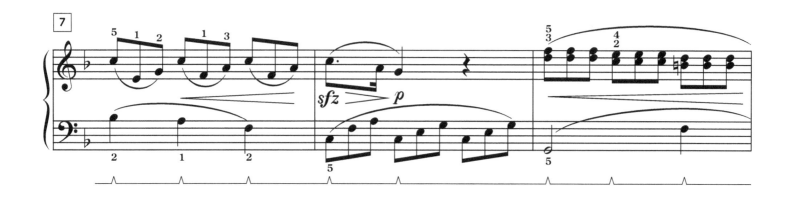

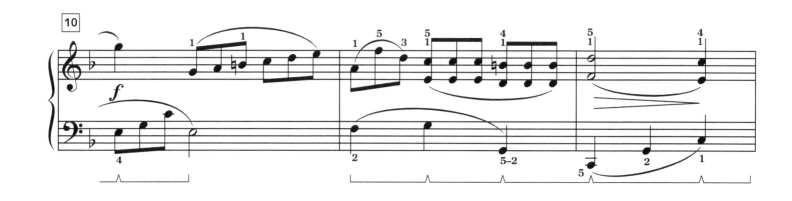

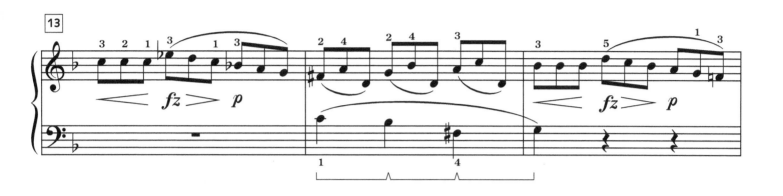

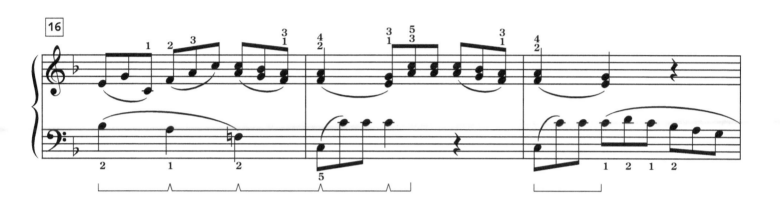

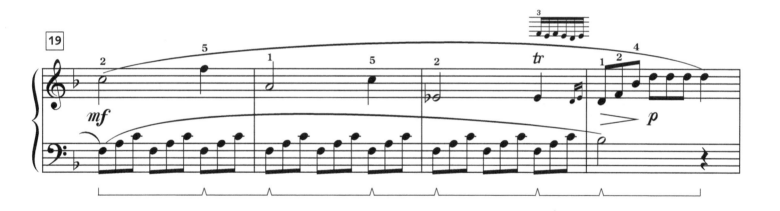

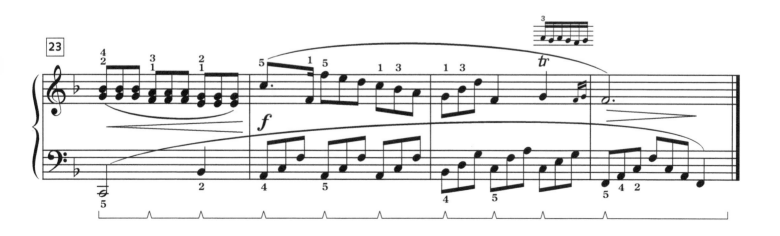

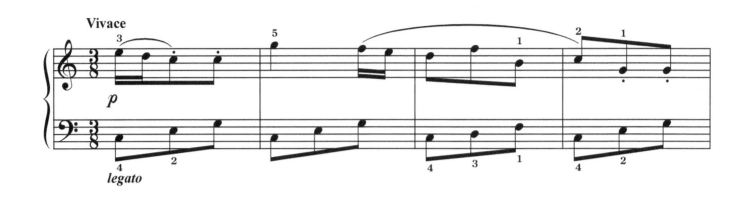

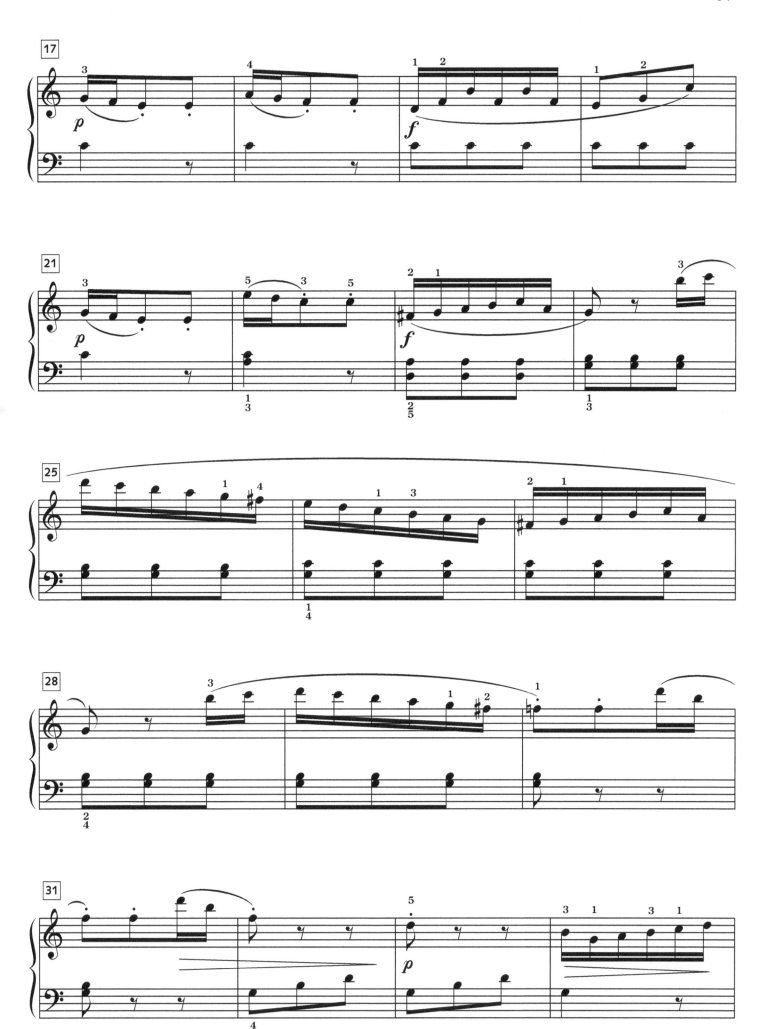

Le Coucou

(The Cuckoo)

Louis-Claude Dacquin
(1694-1772)

First Arabesque

Claude Debussy
(1862-1918)

Tempo rubato (un peu moins vite)

Clair de lune

(Suite bergamasque)

Claude Debussy
(1862-1918)

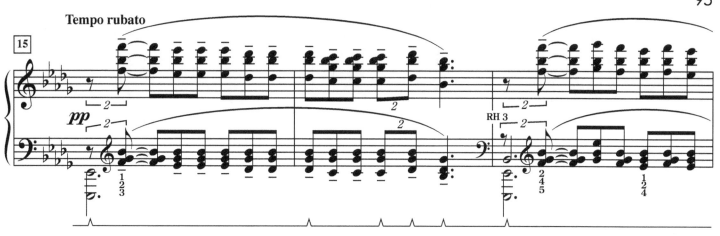

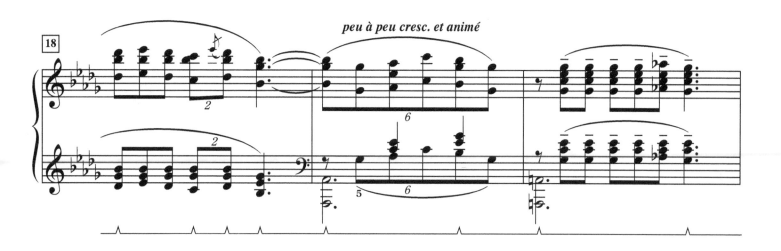

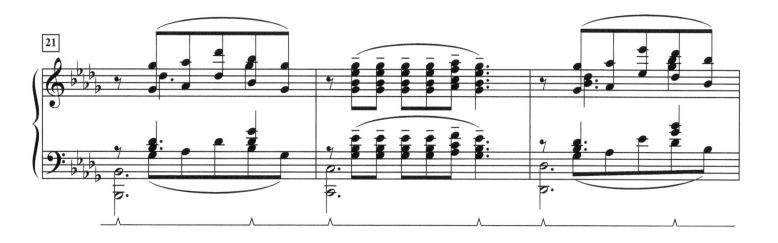

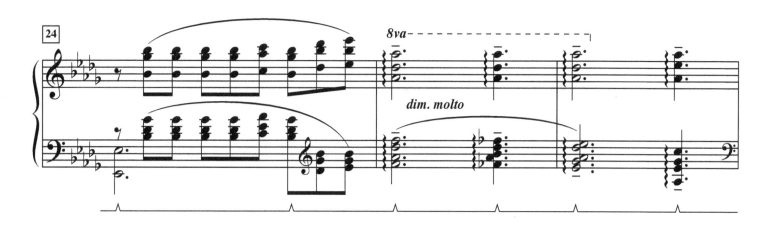

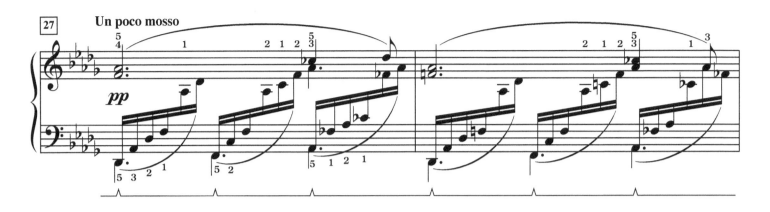

Un poco mosso

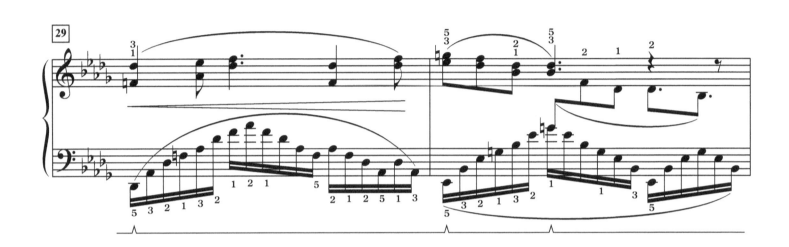

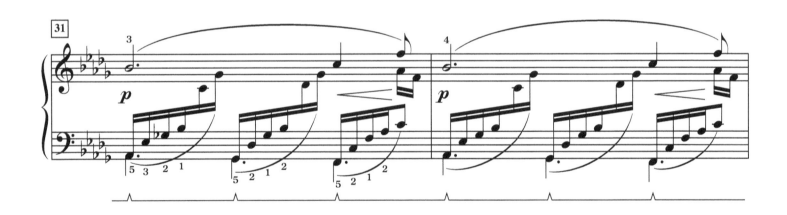

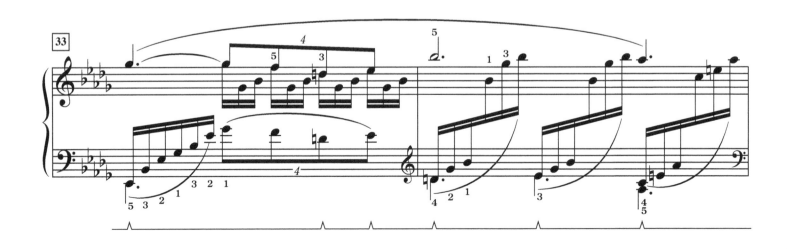

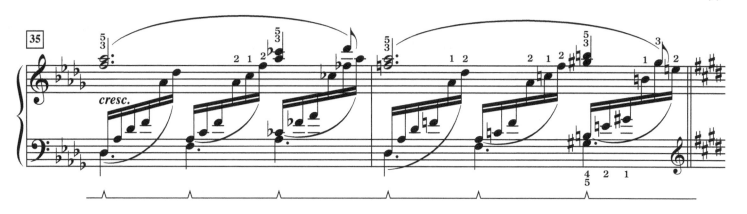

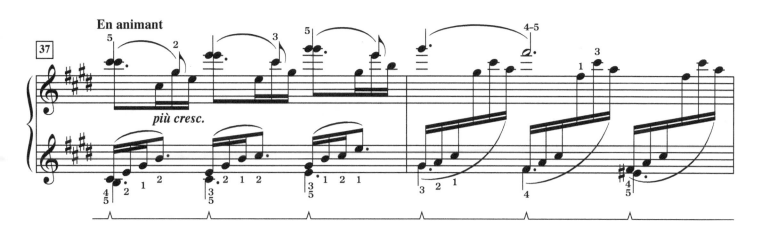

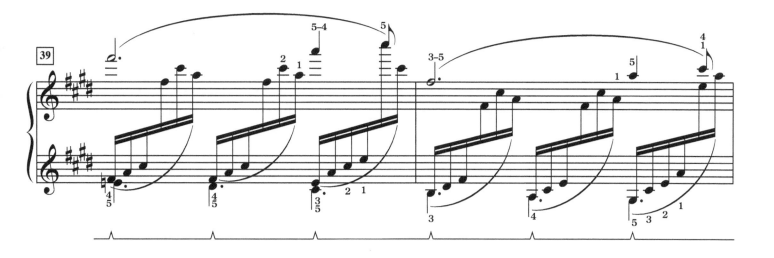

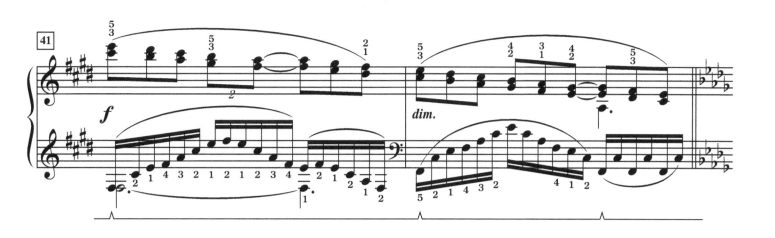

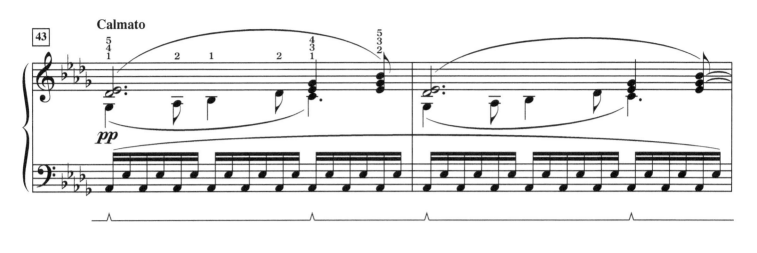

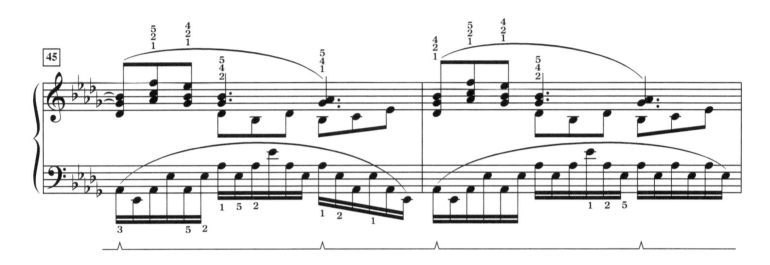

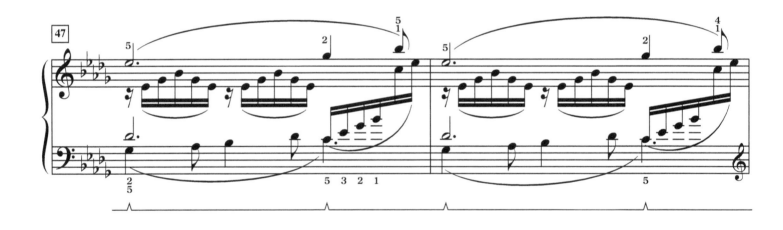

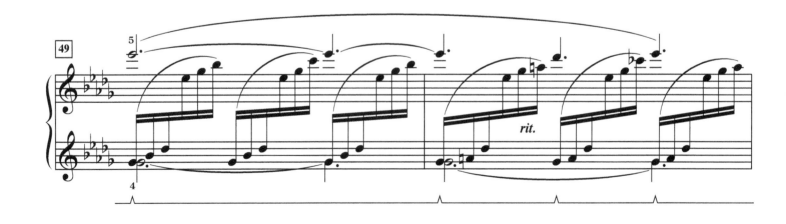

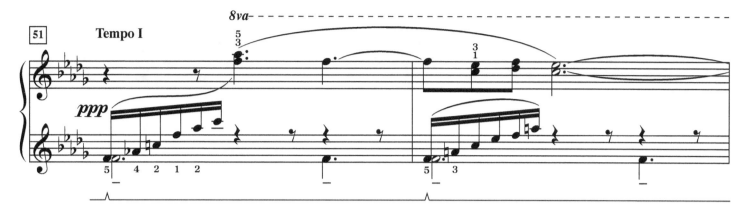

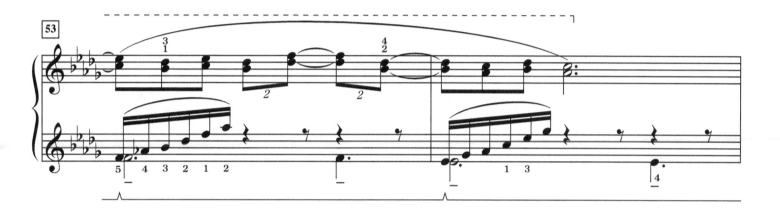

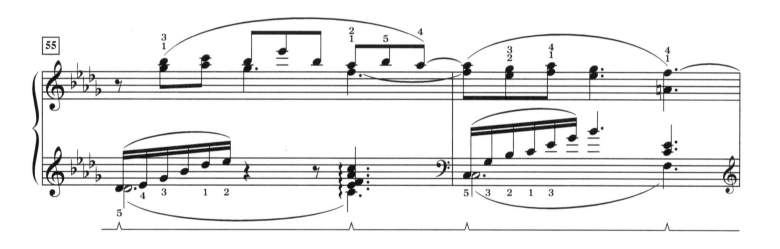

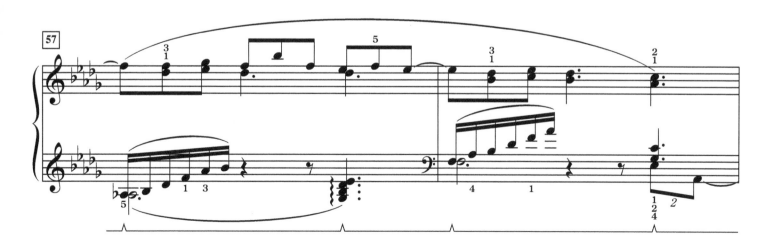

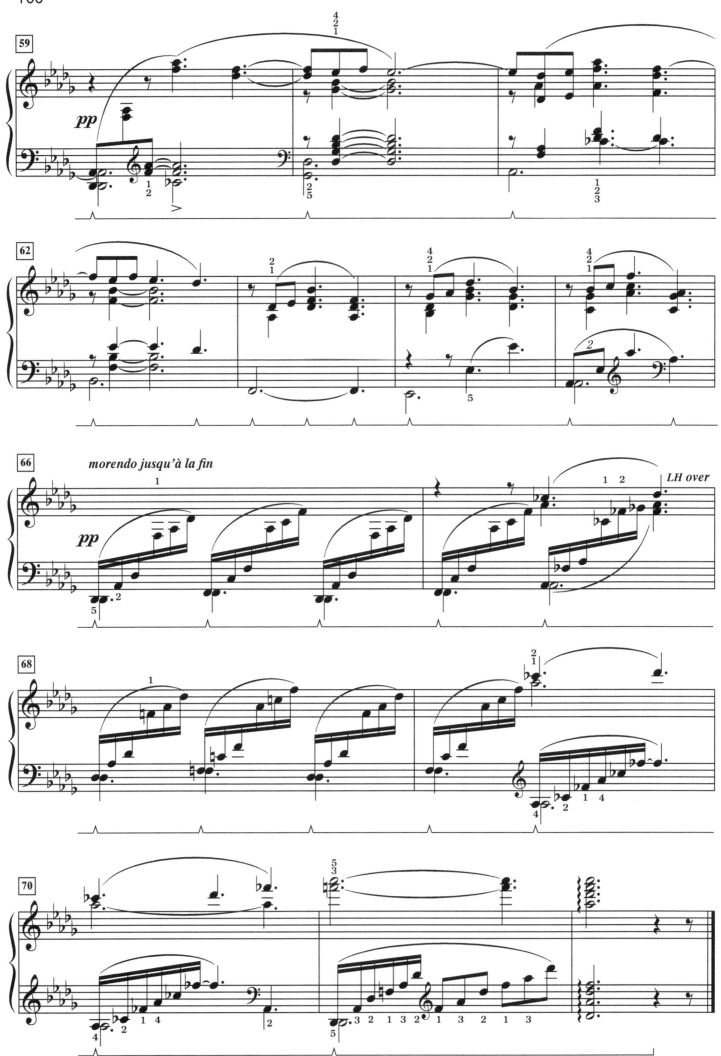

Le fille aux cheveux de lin

(Preludes, Book 1)

Claude Debussy
(1862-1918)

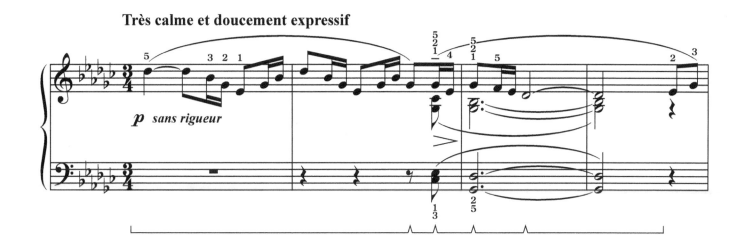

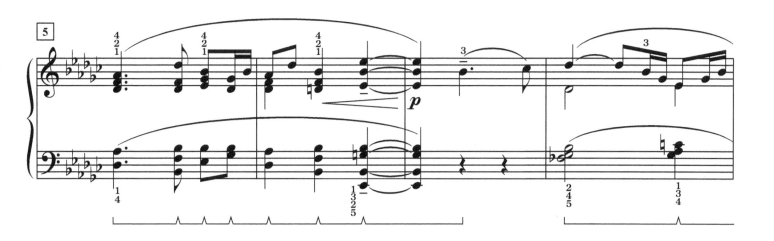

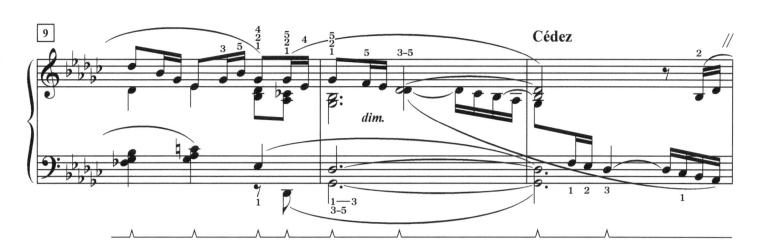

Le petit nègre

Claude Debussy
(1862-1918)

Golliwog's Cakewalk

(Children's Corner)

Claude Debussy
(1862-1918)

Nocturne in B-flat Major

John Field
(1782-1837)

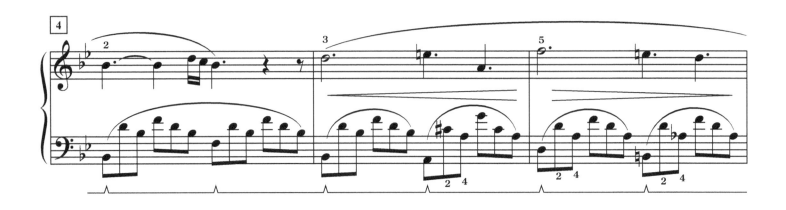

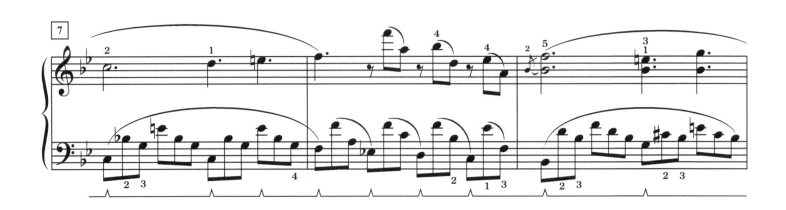

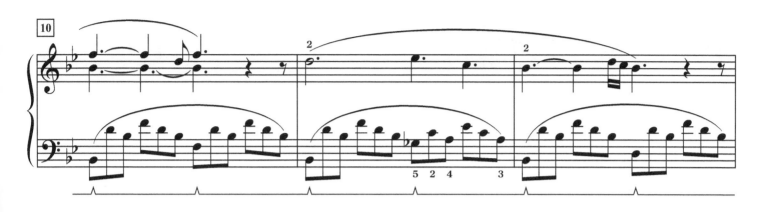

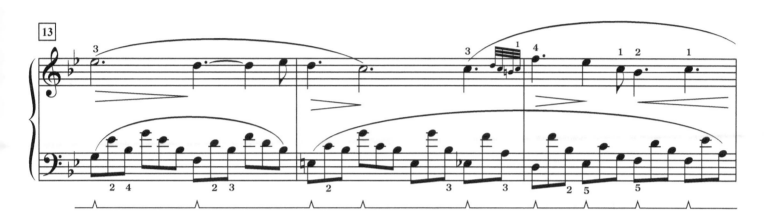

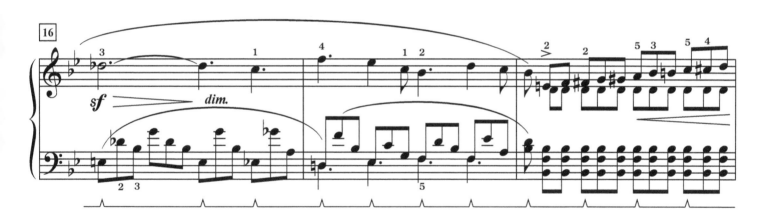

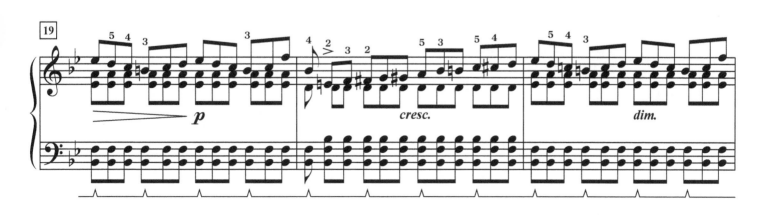

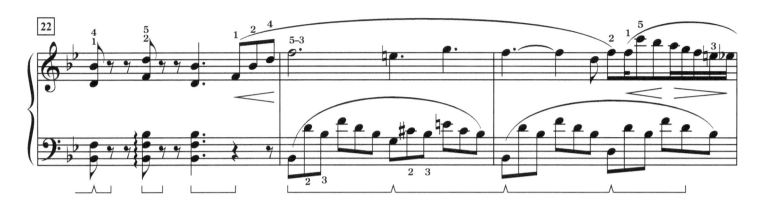

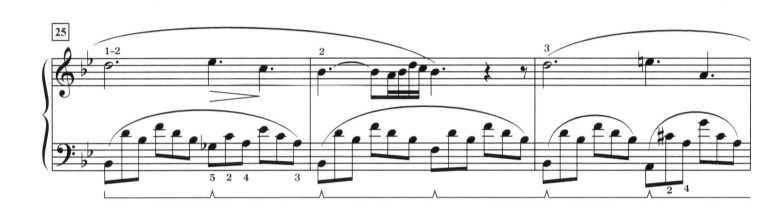

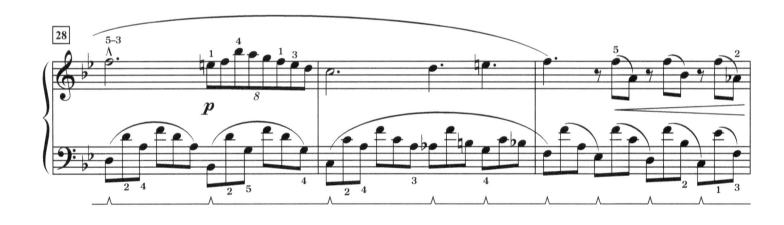

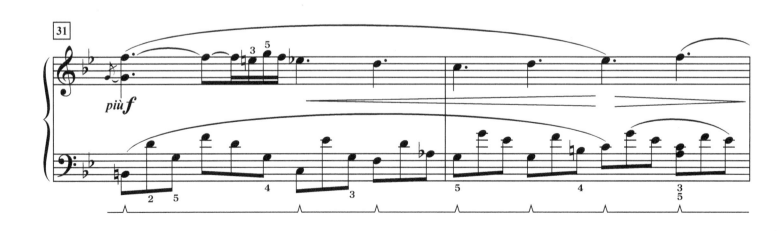

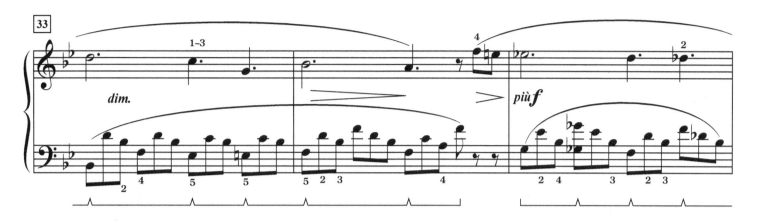

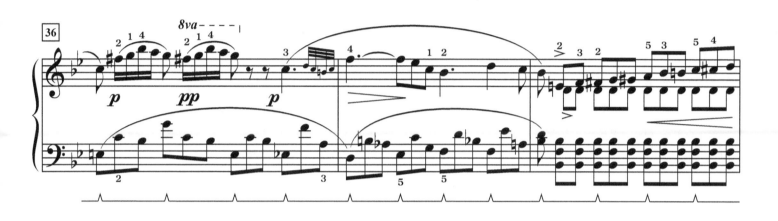

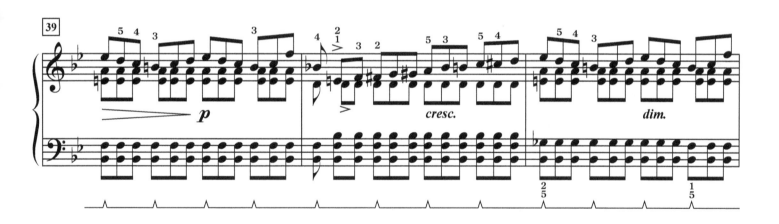

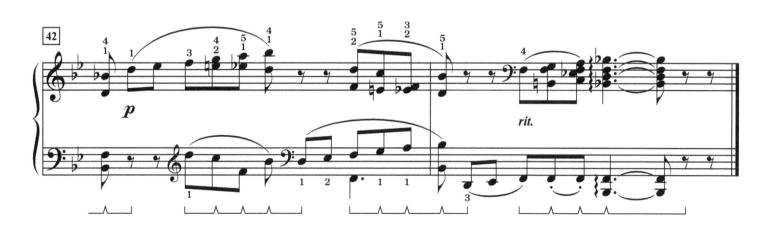

Spanish Dance

Enrique Granados (1867-1916)
Op. 5, No. 5

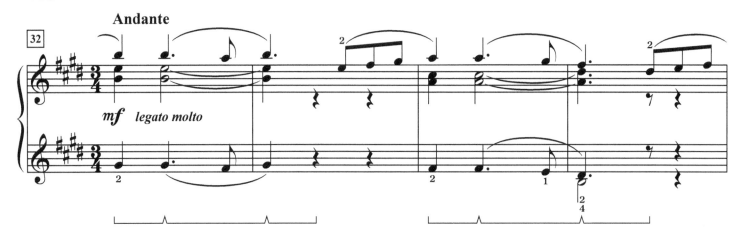

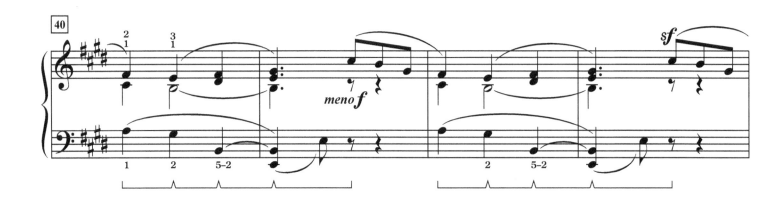

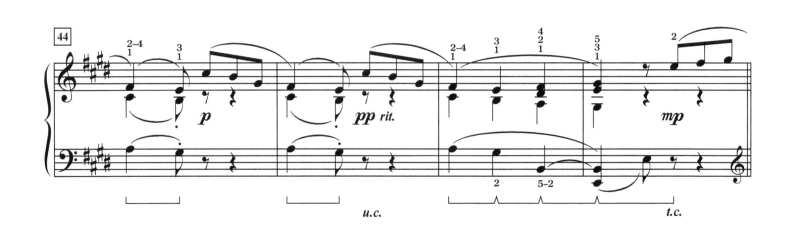

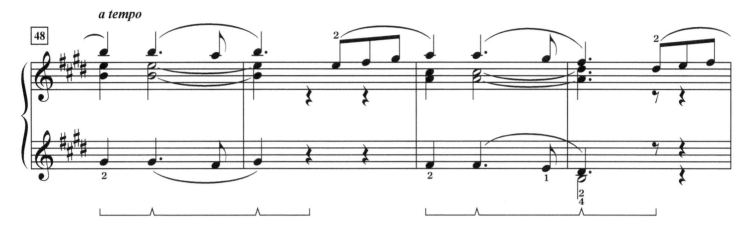

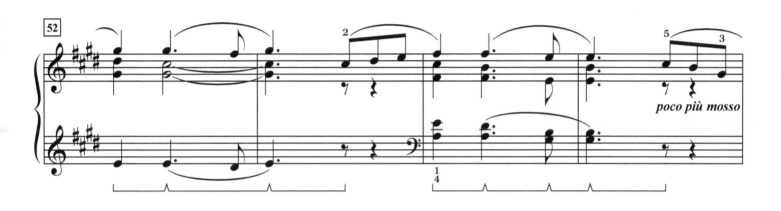

Spinning Song

Albert Ellmenreich (1816-1905)
Op. 14, No. 4

Elfin Dance

Edvard Grieg (1843-1907)
Op. 12, No. 4

Puck

Edvard Grieg (1843-1907)
Op. 71, No. 3

Notturno

Edvard Grieg (1843-1907)
Op. 54, No. 4

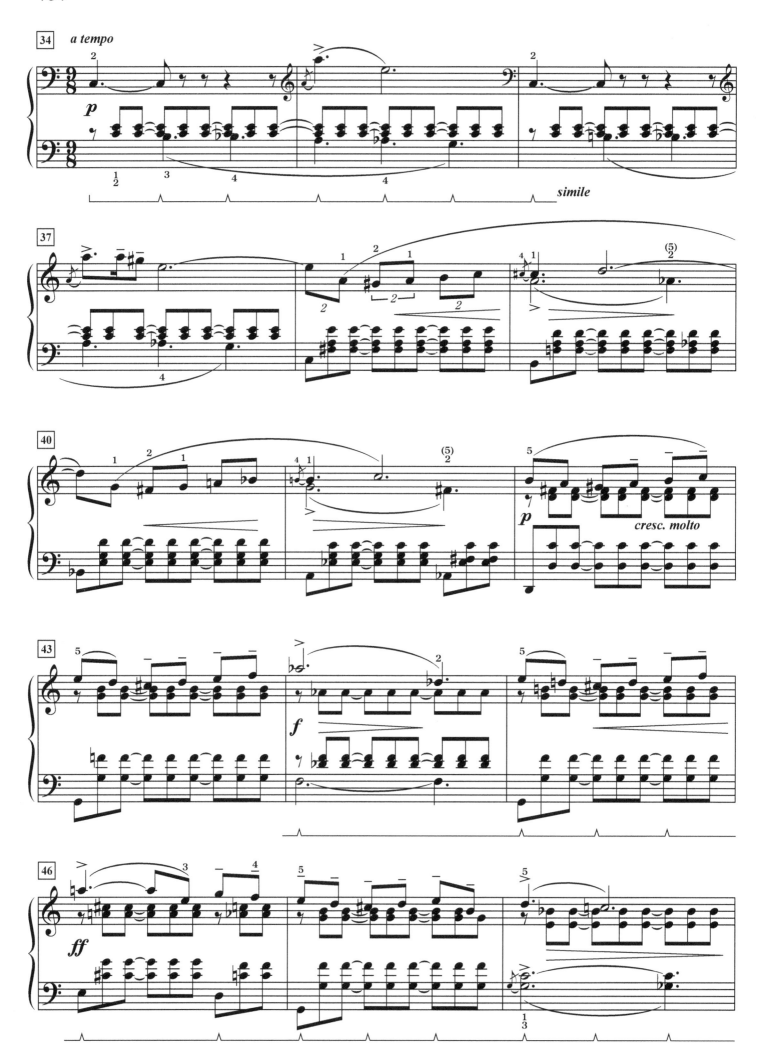

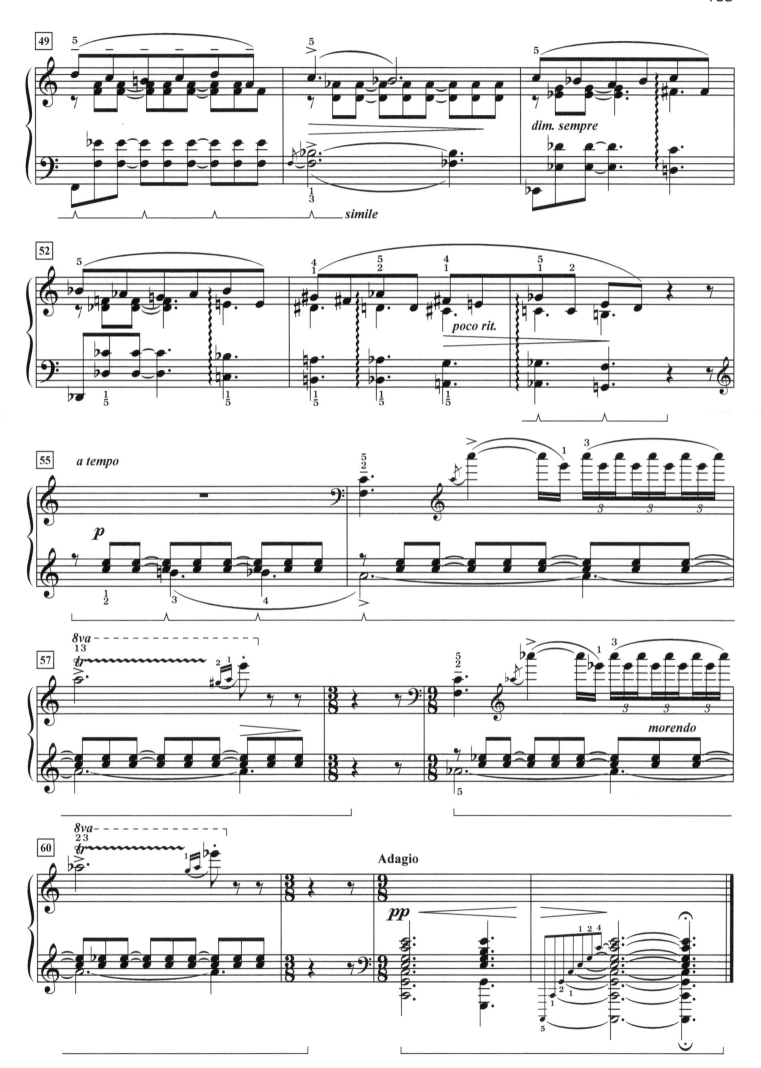

Sarabande
(Suite No. 4 in D Minor)

George Frideric Handel
(1685-1759)

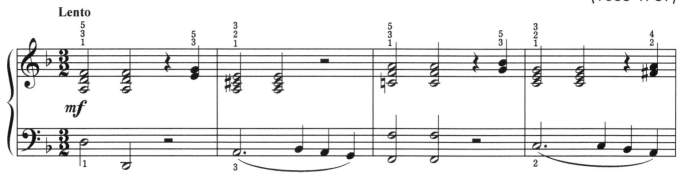

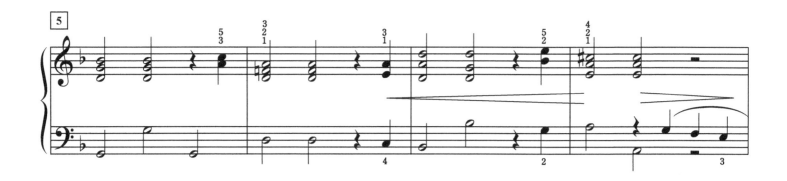

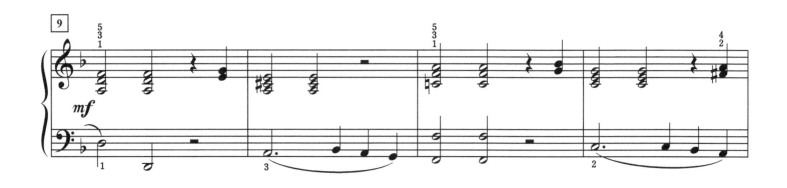

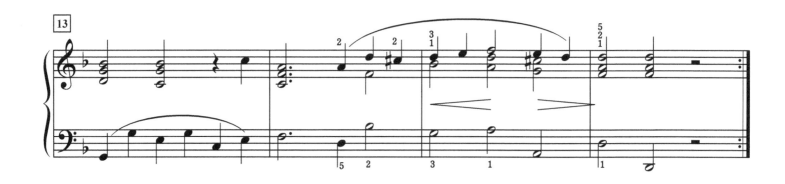

Variation I

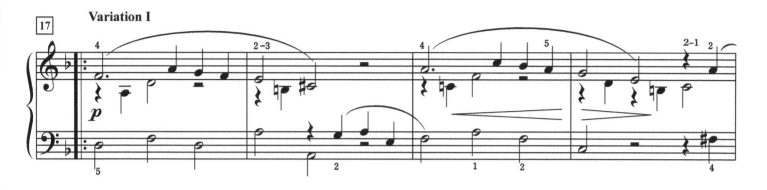

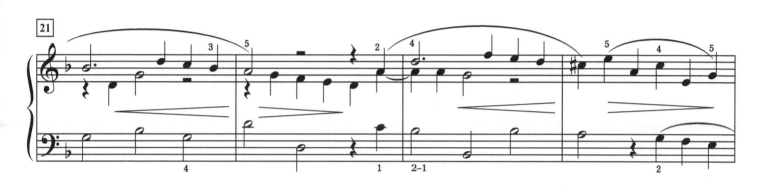

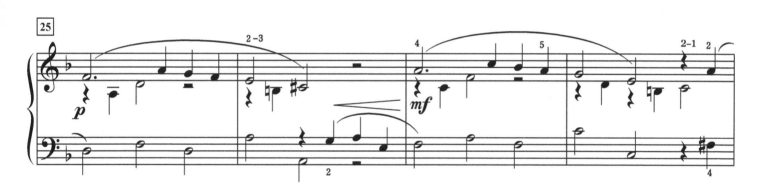

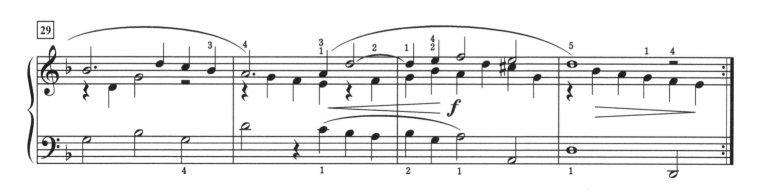

Variation II

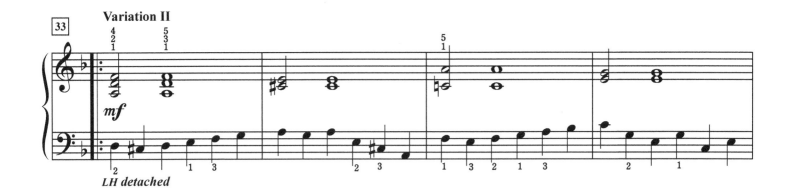

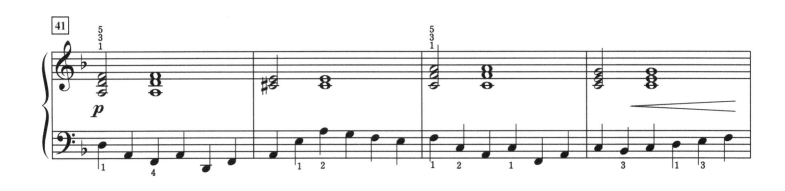

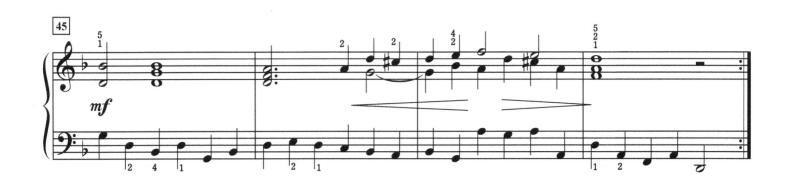

Sonata in C Major

(Movement I)

Franz Joseph Haydn (1732-1809)
Hob. XVI/35

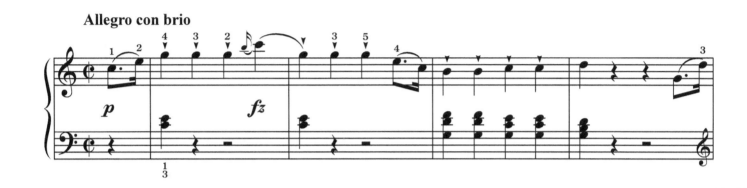

Sonata in D Major

(Movement I)

Franz Joseph Haydn (1732-1809)
Hob. XVI/37

Allegro con brio

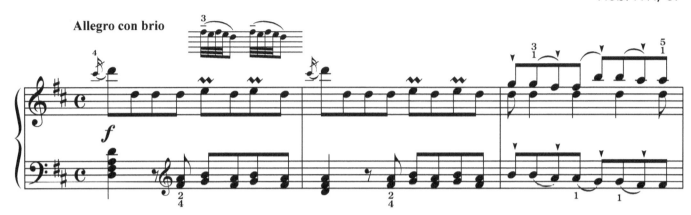

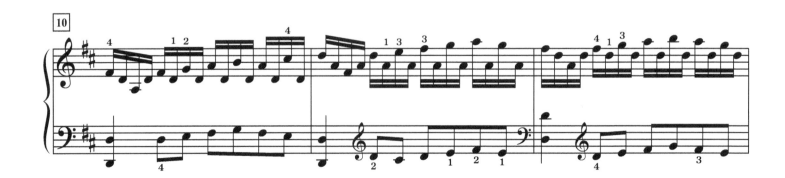

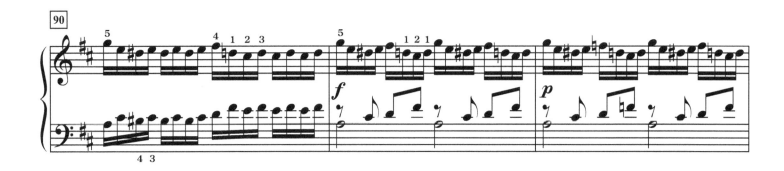

The Little White Donkey

(Histoires)

Jacques Ibert
(1890-1962)

Avec une tranquille bonne humeur

Un peu ralenti

Avec la même humeur paisible du début

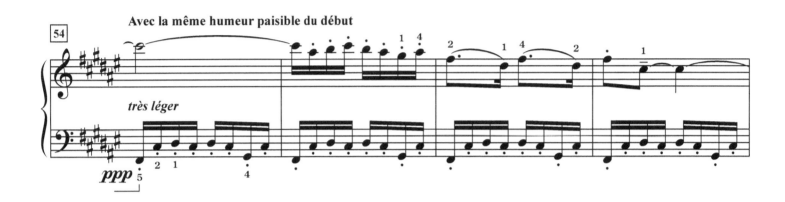

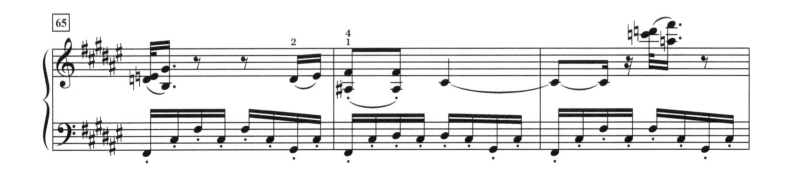

A Giddy Girl

(Histoires)

Jacques Ibert
(1890-1962)

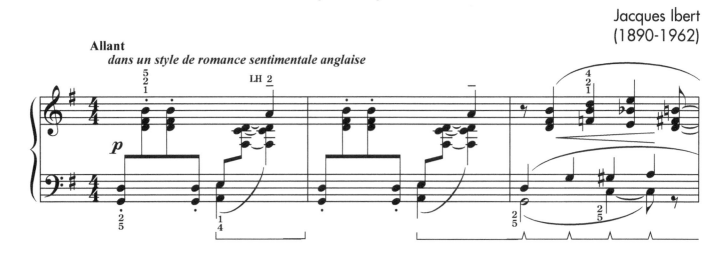

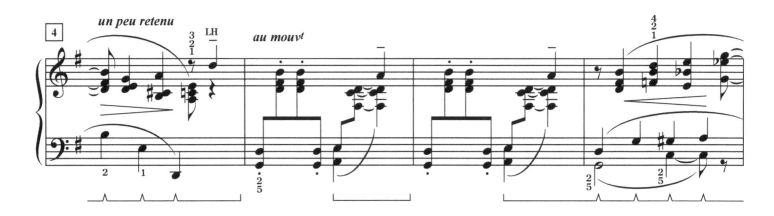

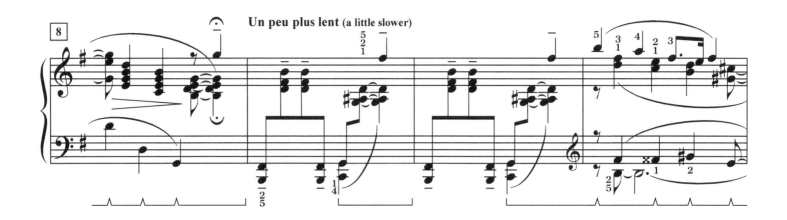

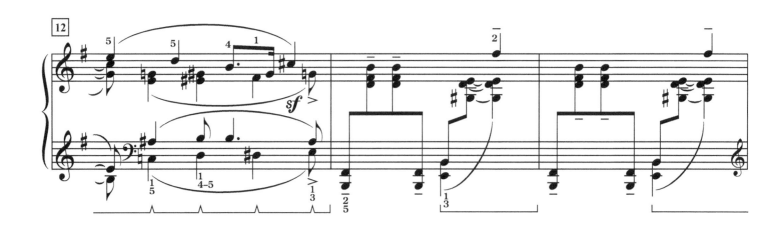

The Avalanche

Stephen Heller (1813-1888)
Op. 45, No. 2

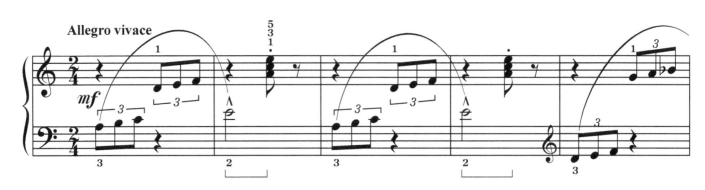

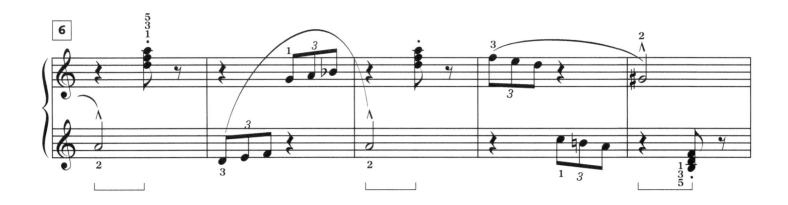

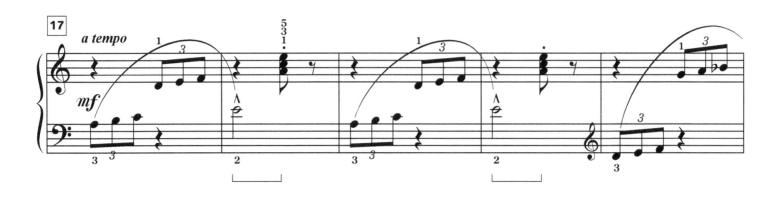

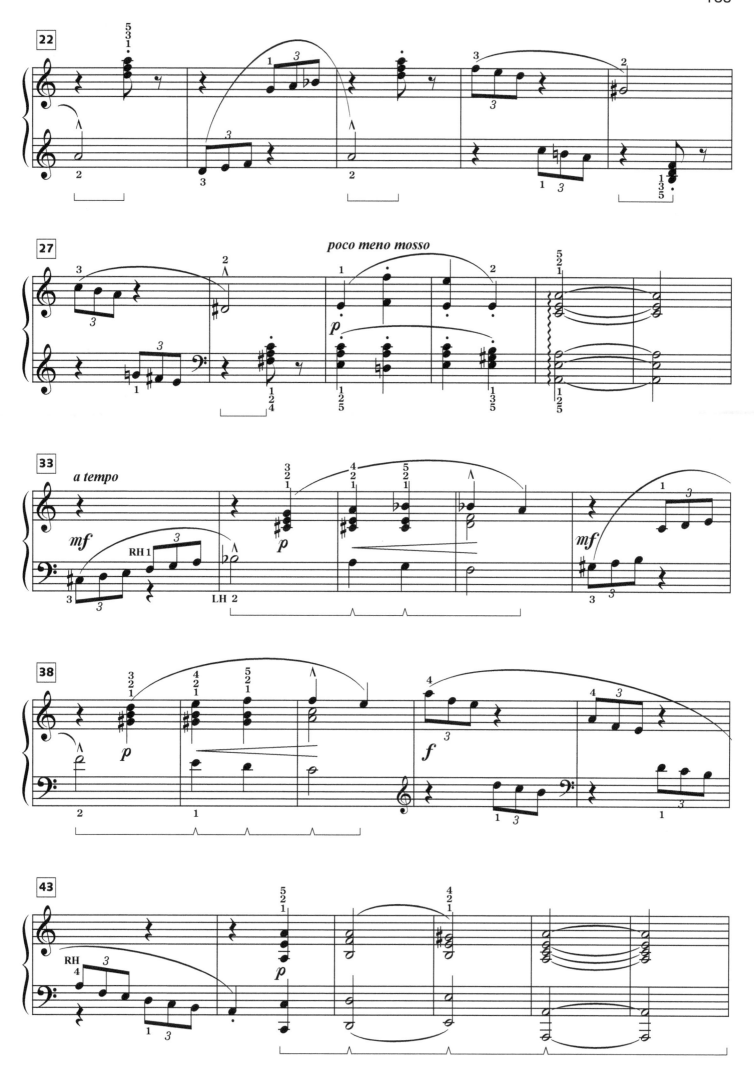

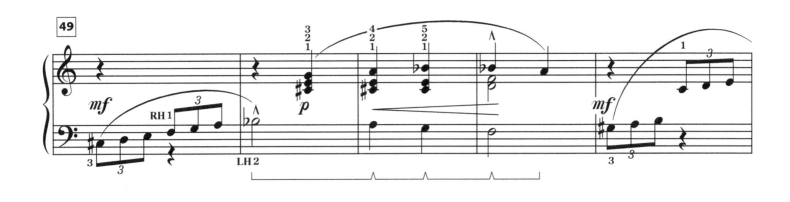

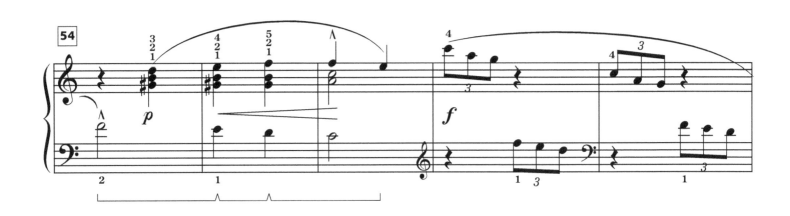

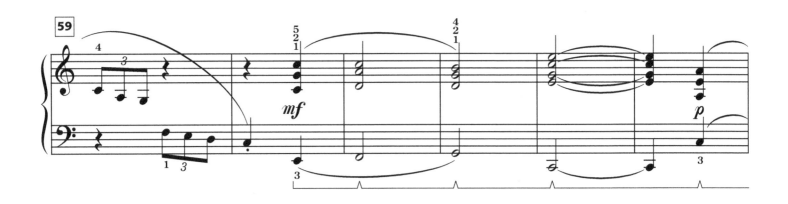

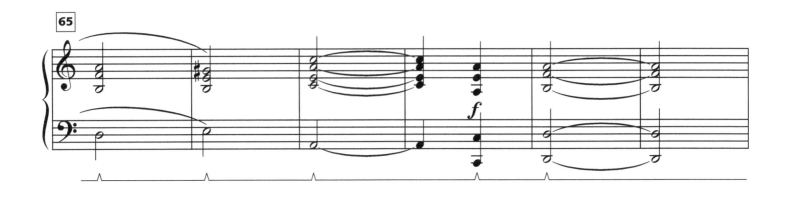

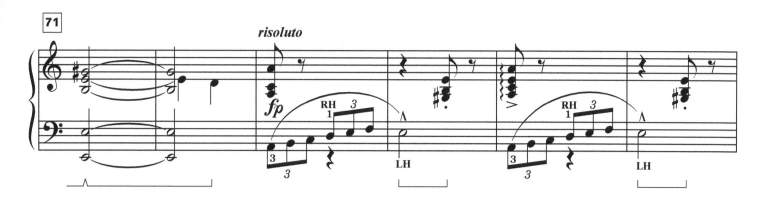

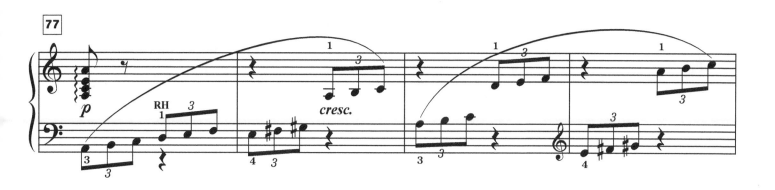

The Easy Winners

Scott Joplin
(1868-1917)

The Entertainer

Scott Joplin
(1868-1917)

Maple Leaf Rag

Scott Joplin
(1868-1917)

Sonatina in C Major

(Movements I & II)

Friedrich Kuhlau (1786-1832)
Op. 55, No. 3

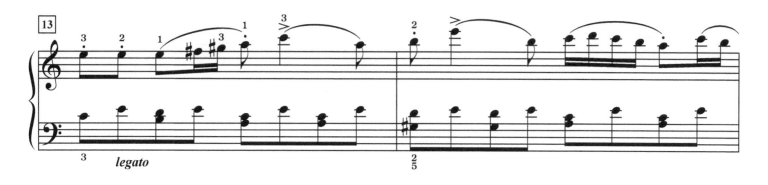

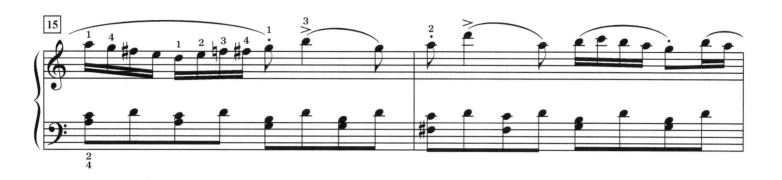

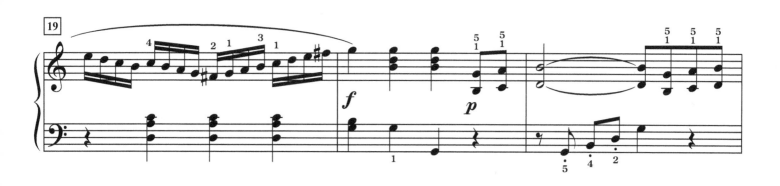

Allegretto grazioso

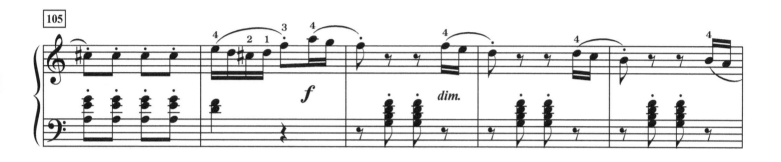

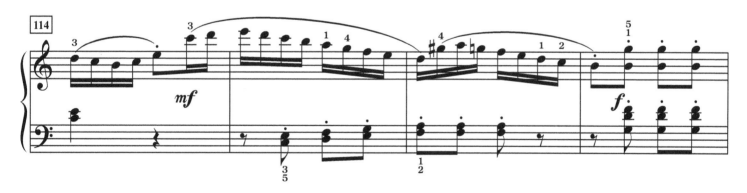

To a Wild Rose
(Woodland Sketches)

Edward MacDowell (1861-1908)
Op. 51, No. 1

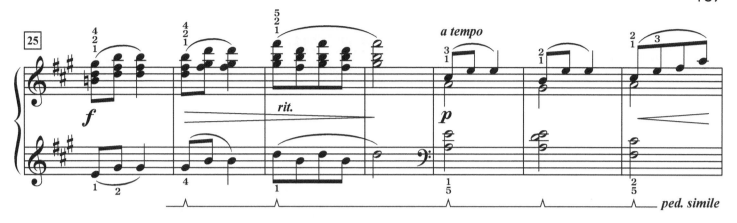

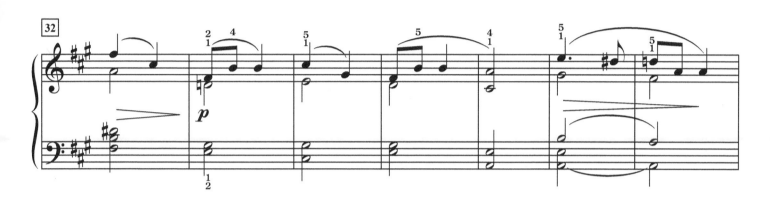

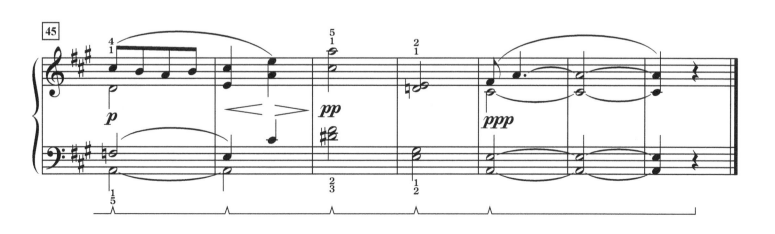

Consolation
(Songs without Words)

Felix Mendelssohn (1809-1847)
Op. 30, No. 3

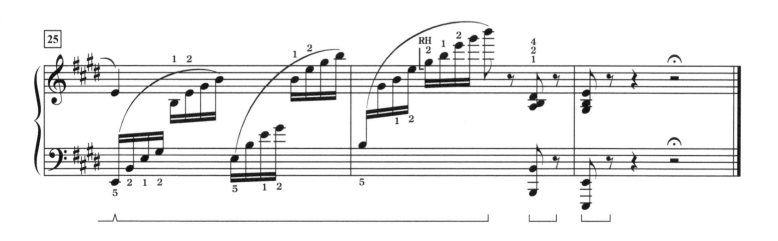

Venetian Boat Song
(Songs without Words)

Felix Mendelssohn (1809-1847)
Op. 19, No. 6

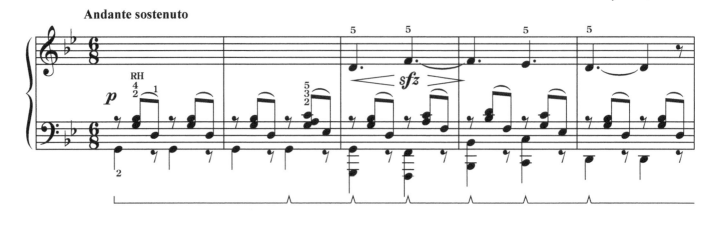

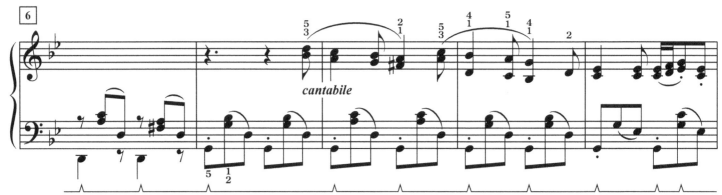

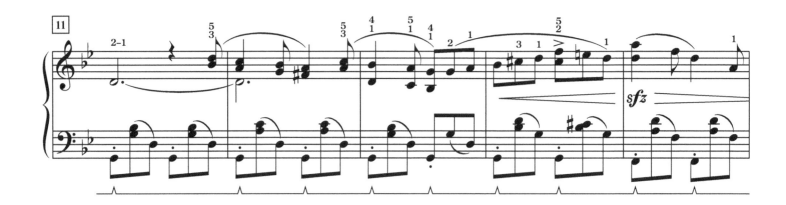

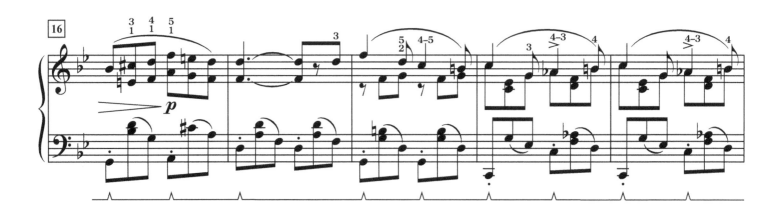

Venetian Boat Song
(Songs without Words)

Felix Mendelssohn (1809-1847)
Op. 30, No. 6

Spanish Dance

Moritz Moszkowski (1854-1925)
Op. 12, No. 1

Fantasy in D Minor

Wolfgang Amadeus Mozart (1756-1791)
K. 397

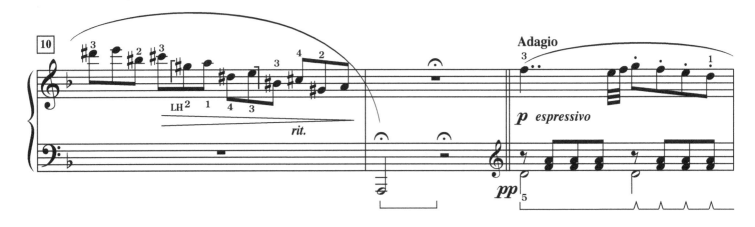

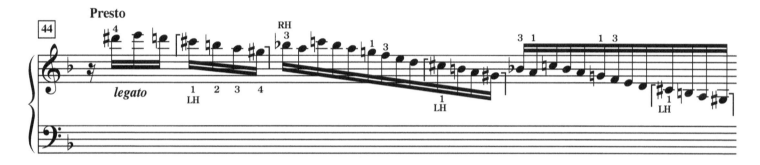

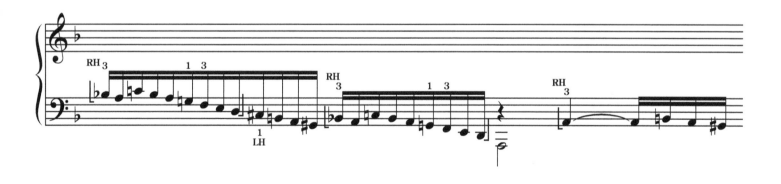

Sonata in C Major
(Movement I)

Wolfgang Amadeus Mozart (1756-1791)

K. 545

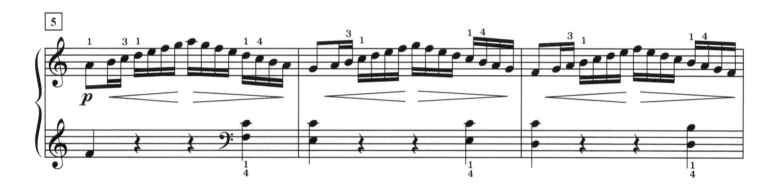

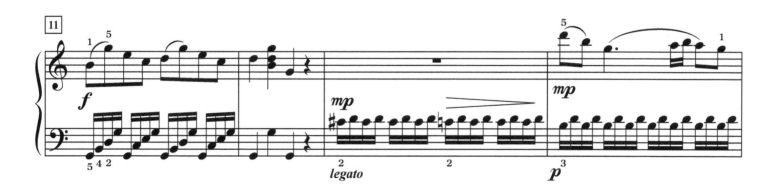

Sonata in A Major

(Rondo Alla Turca)

(Movement III)

Wolfgang Amadeus Mozart (1756-1791)

K. 331

Alla turca
Allegretto

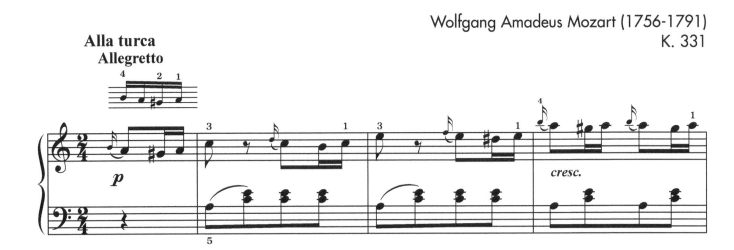

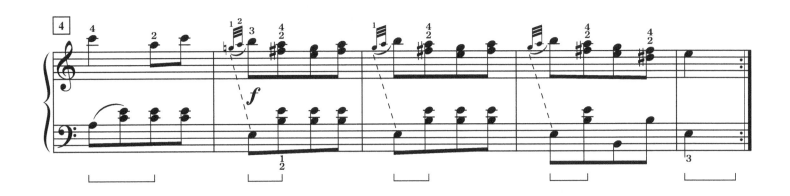

Minuet in G Major

Ignace Paderewski (1860-1941)
Op. 14, No. 1

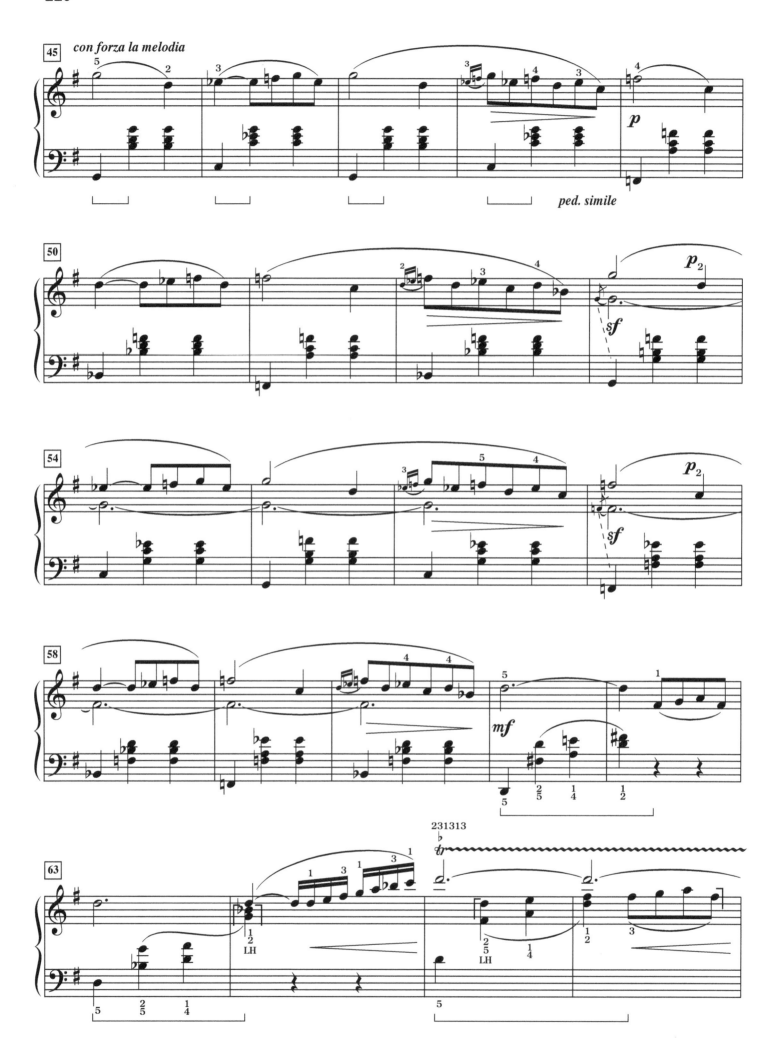

Toccata in A Major

Pietro Paradisi
(1707-1791)

(a) Play eighth notes slightly detached.

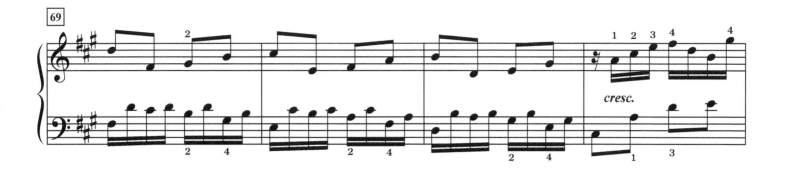

Remando

Ernesto Nazareth
(1863-1934)

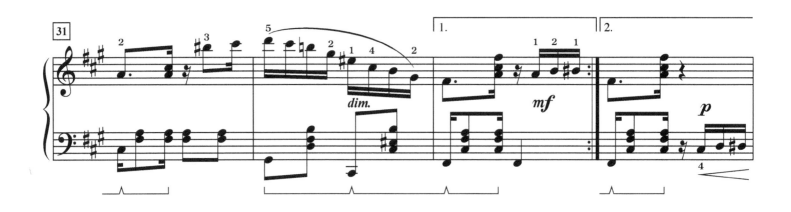

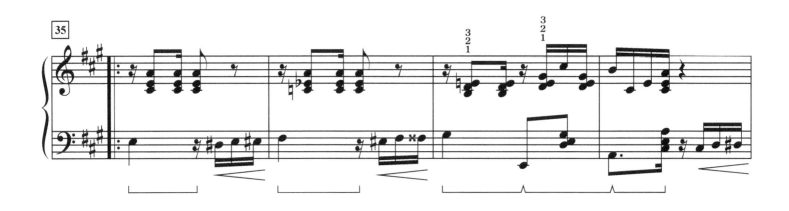

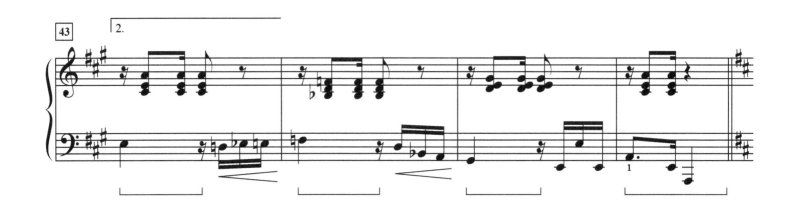

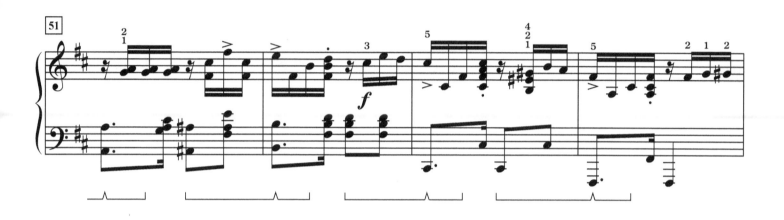

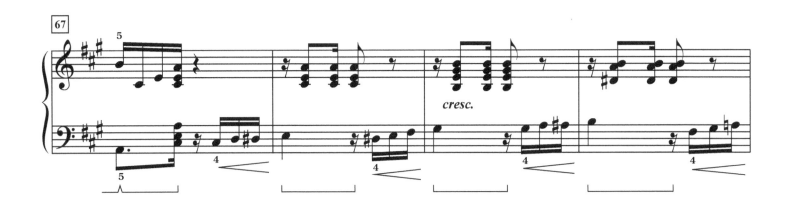

Prelude in C-sharp Minor

Sergei Rachmaninoff (1873-1943)
Op. 3, No. 2

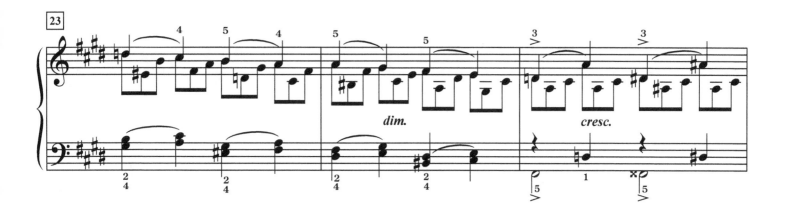

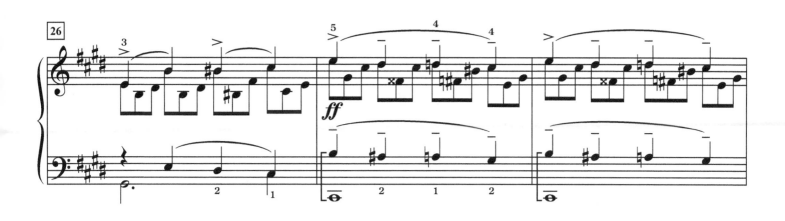

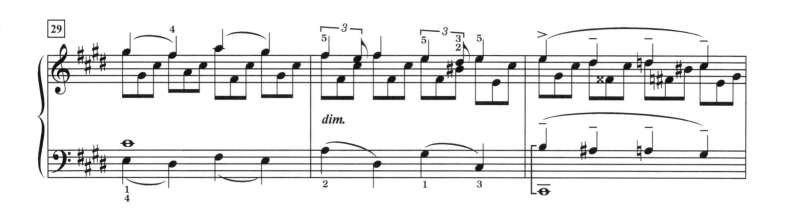

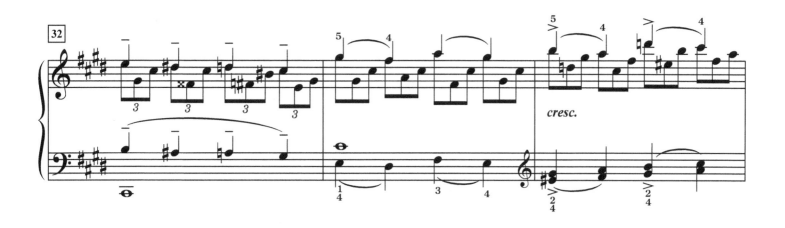

First Gymnopédie

Erik Satie
(1866-1925)

Sonata in A Major
(Movement I)

Franz Schubert (1797-1828)
Op. 120

Allegro moderato

Moments musicaux

Franz Schubert (1797-1828)
Op. 94, No. 3

Impromptu in A-flat Major

Franz Schubert (1797-1828)
Op. 142, No. 2

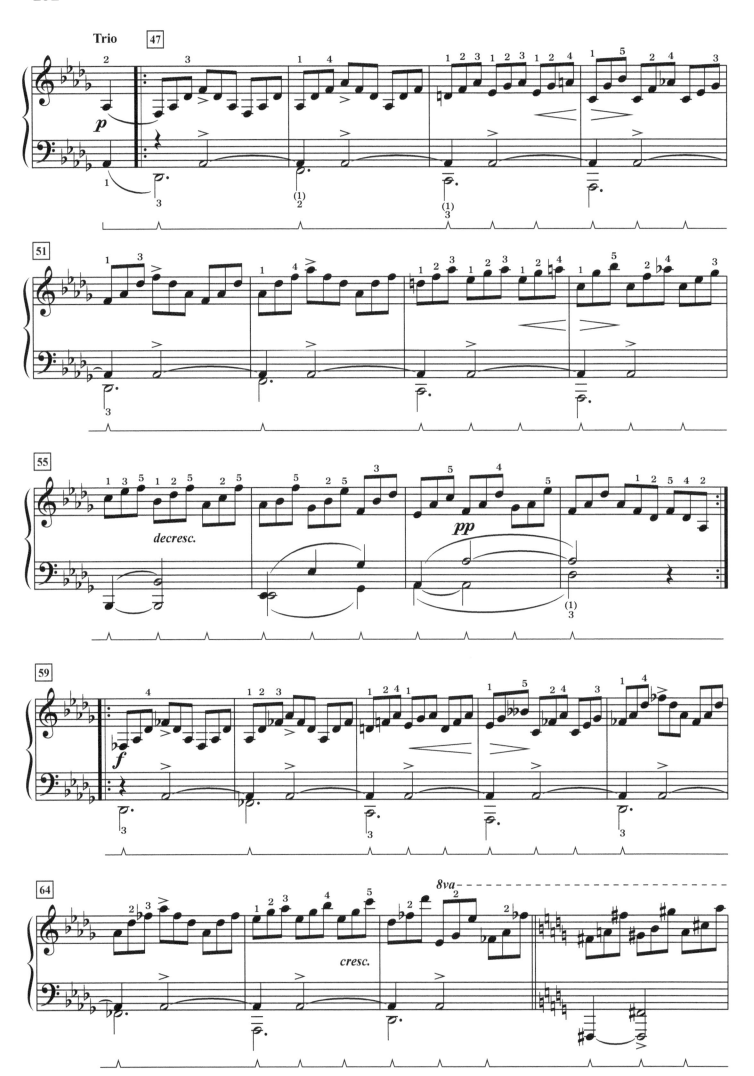

Grillen
(Fantasiestücke)

Robert Schumann (1810-1856)
Op. 12, No. 4

Knecht Ruprecht

(Album for the Young)

Robert Schumann (1810-1856)
Op. 68, No. 12

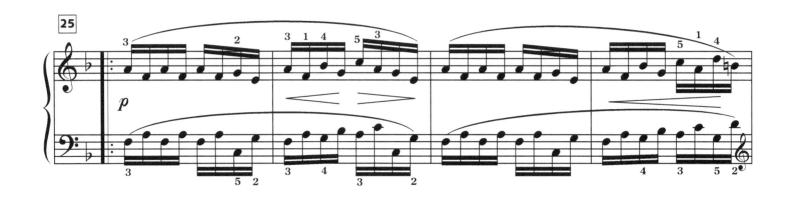

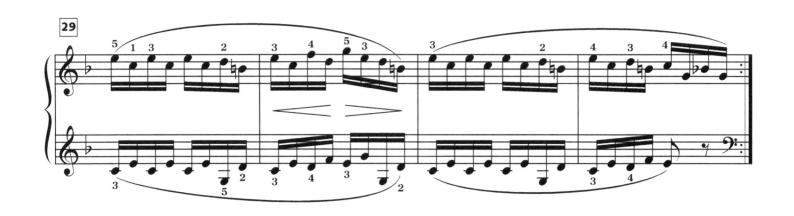

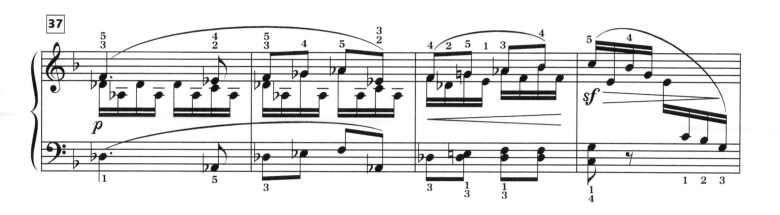

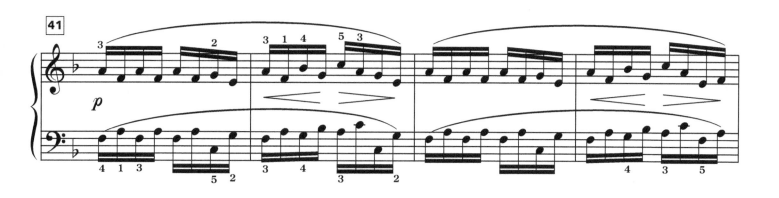

D. C. al Fine
(without repeat)

Träumerei
(Scenes from Childhood)

Robert Schumann (1810-1856)
Op. 15, No. 7

Romance

Jean Sibelius (1865-1952)
Op. 24, No. 9

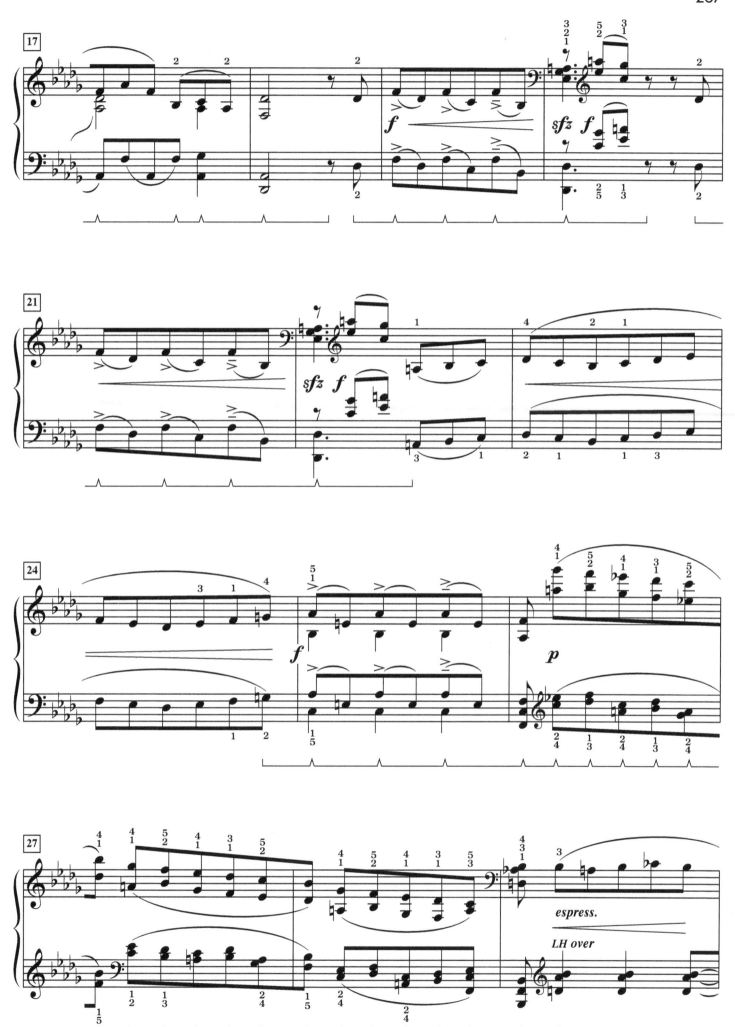

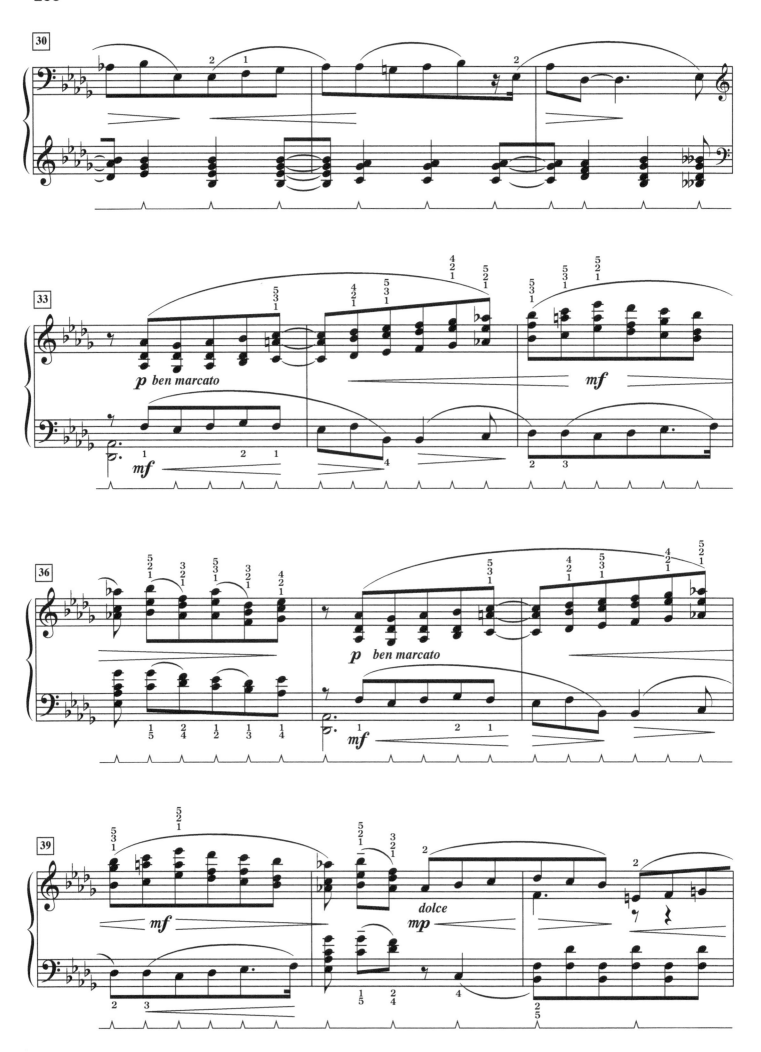

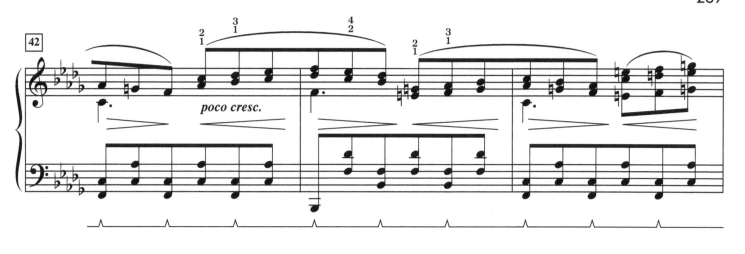

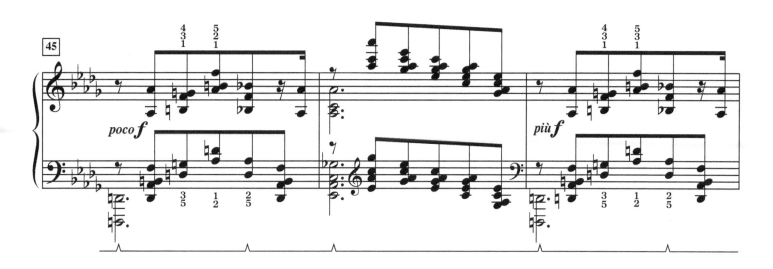

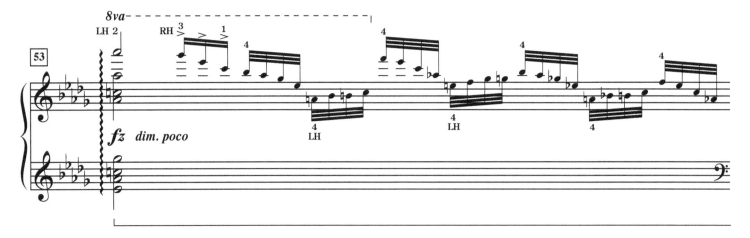

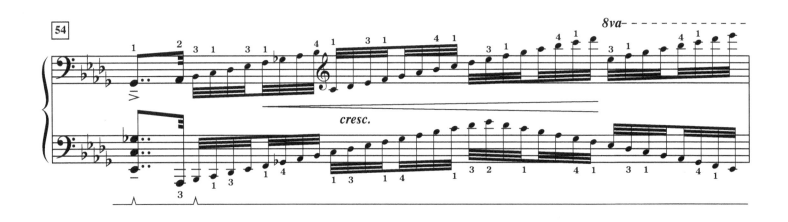

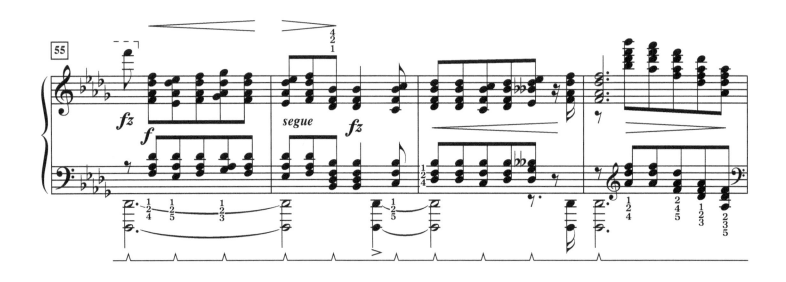

Rustles of Spring

Christian Sinding (1856-1941)
Op. 32, No. 3

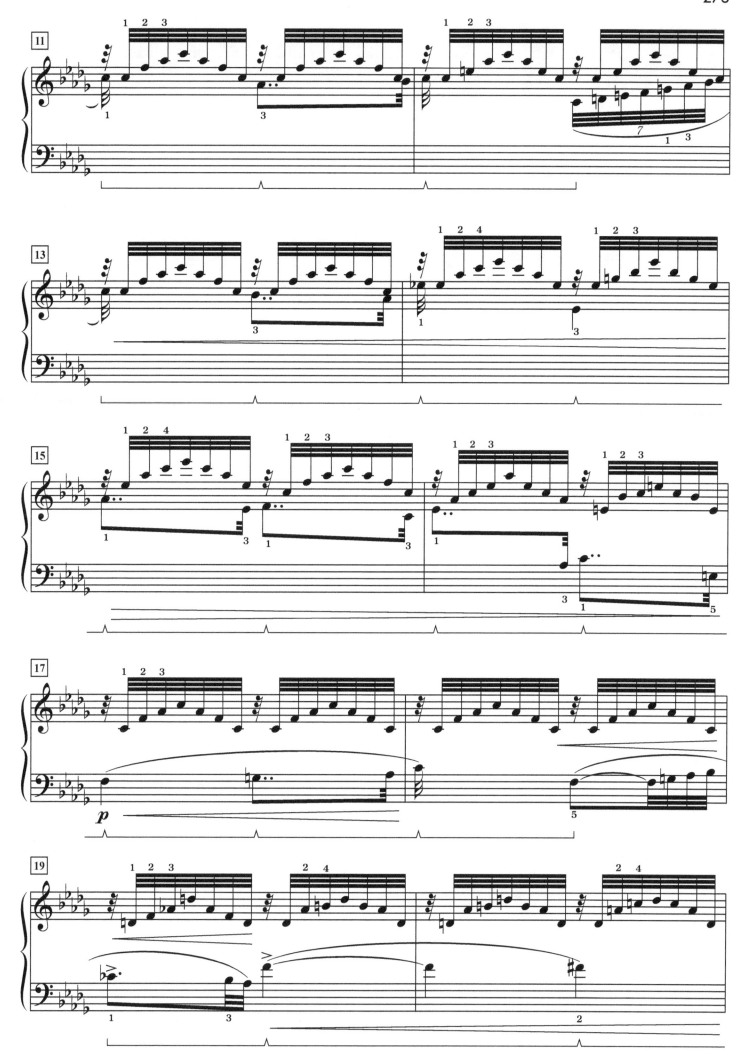

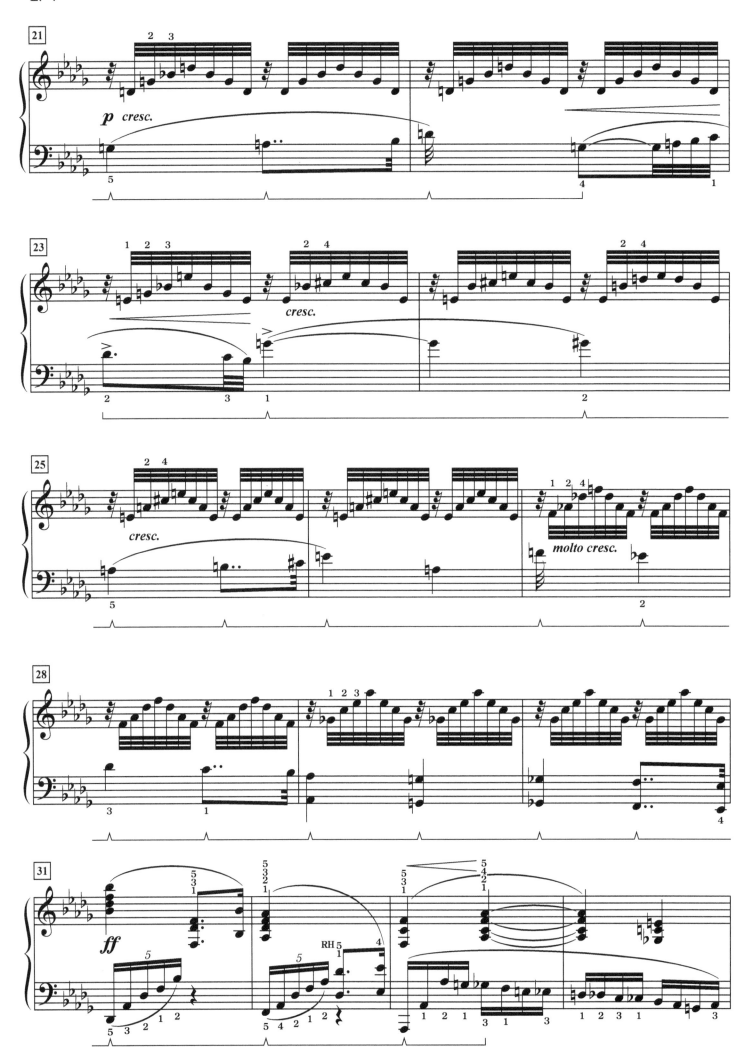

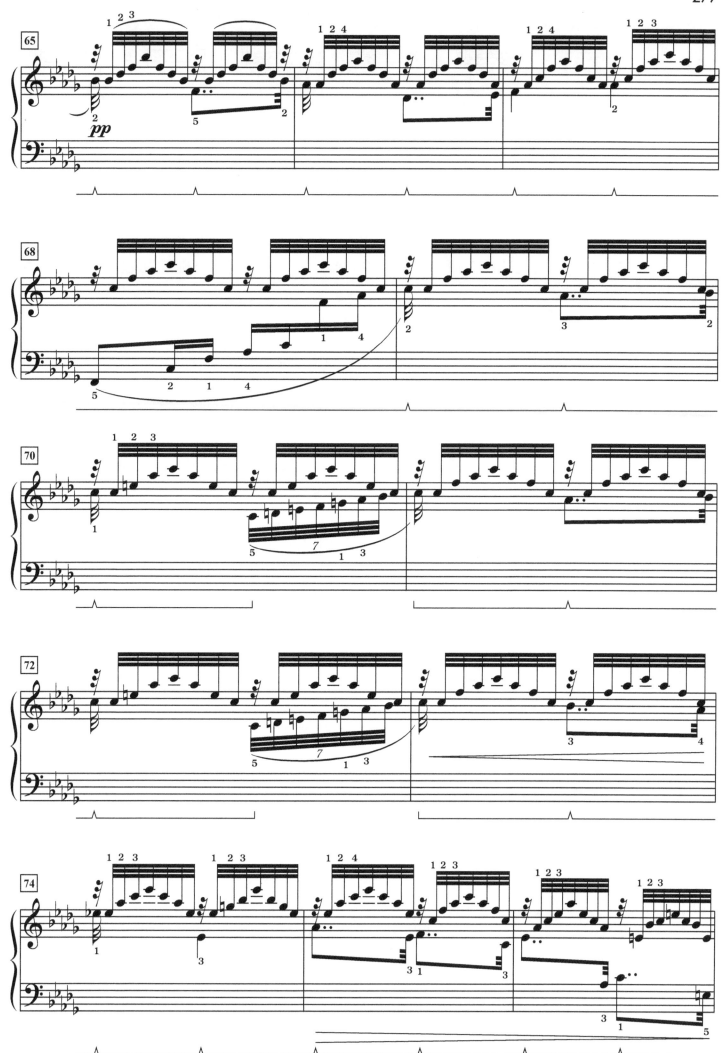

Bagatelle

Alexander Tcherepnin (1899-1977)
Op. 5, No. 10

O Polichinelo

(The Baby's Family, Book 1)

Heitor Villa-Lobos
(1887-1959)

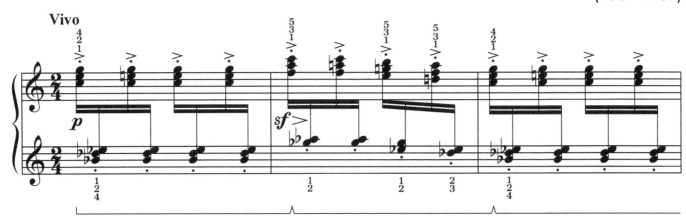

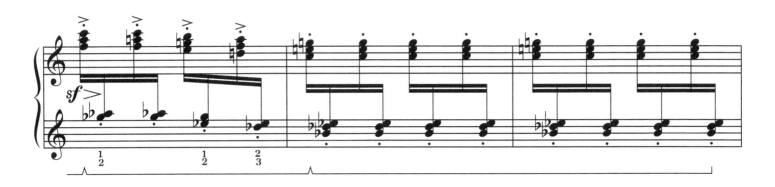

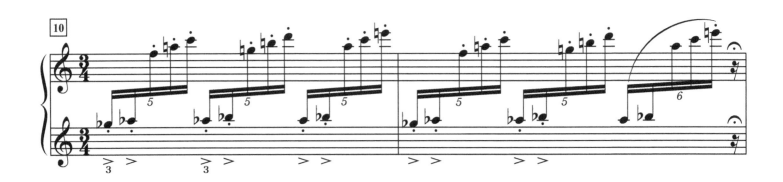

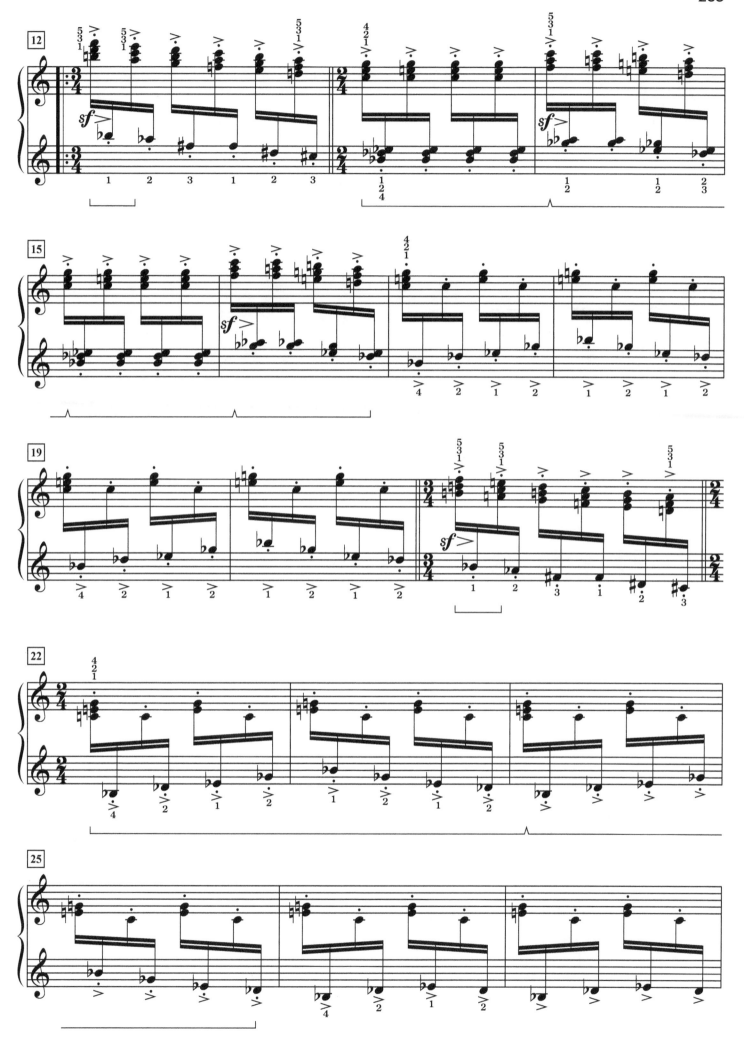

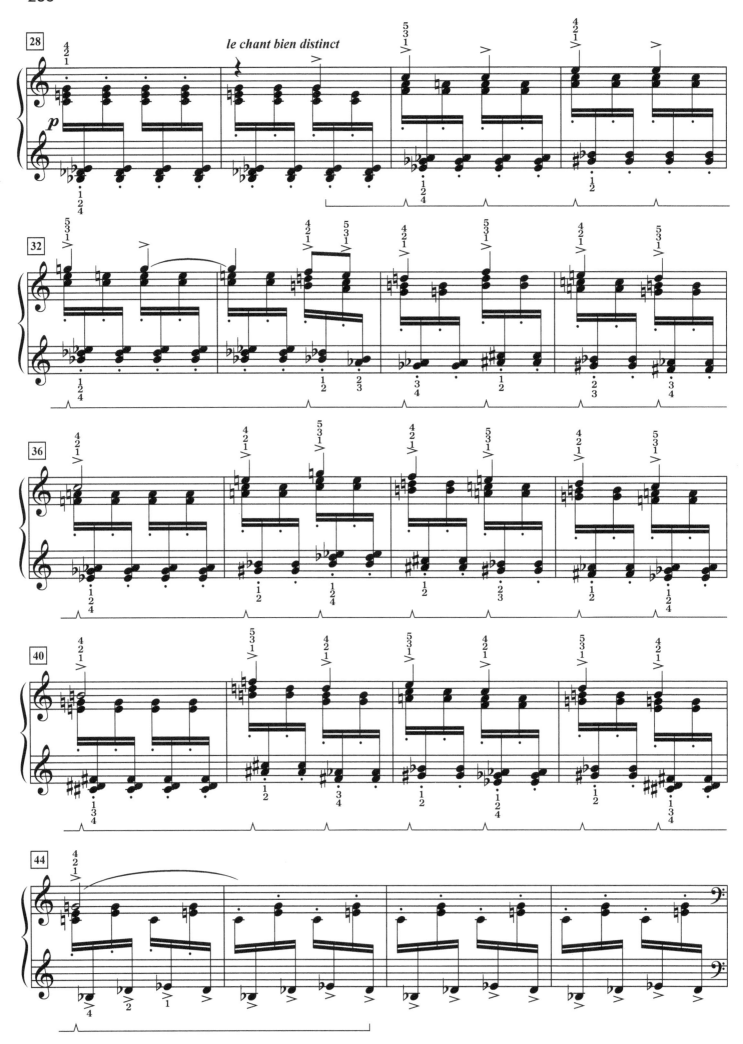

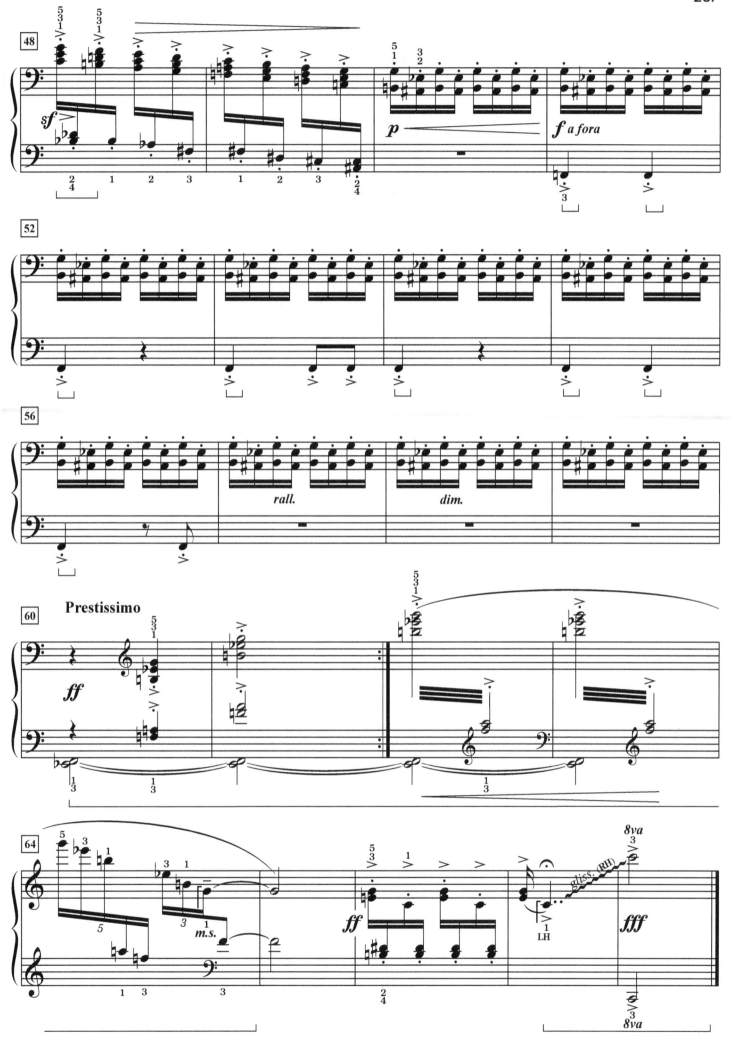

Fughetta

Domenico Zipoli
(1688-1726)